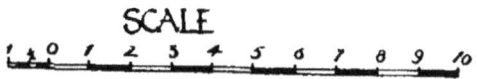

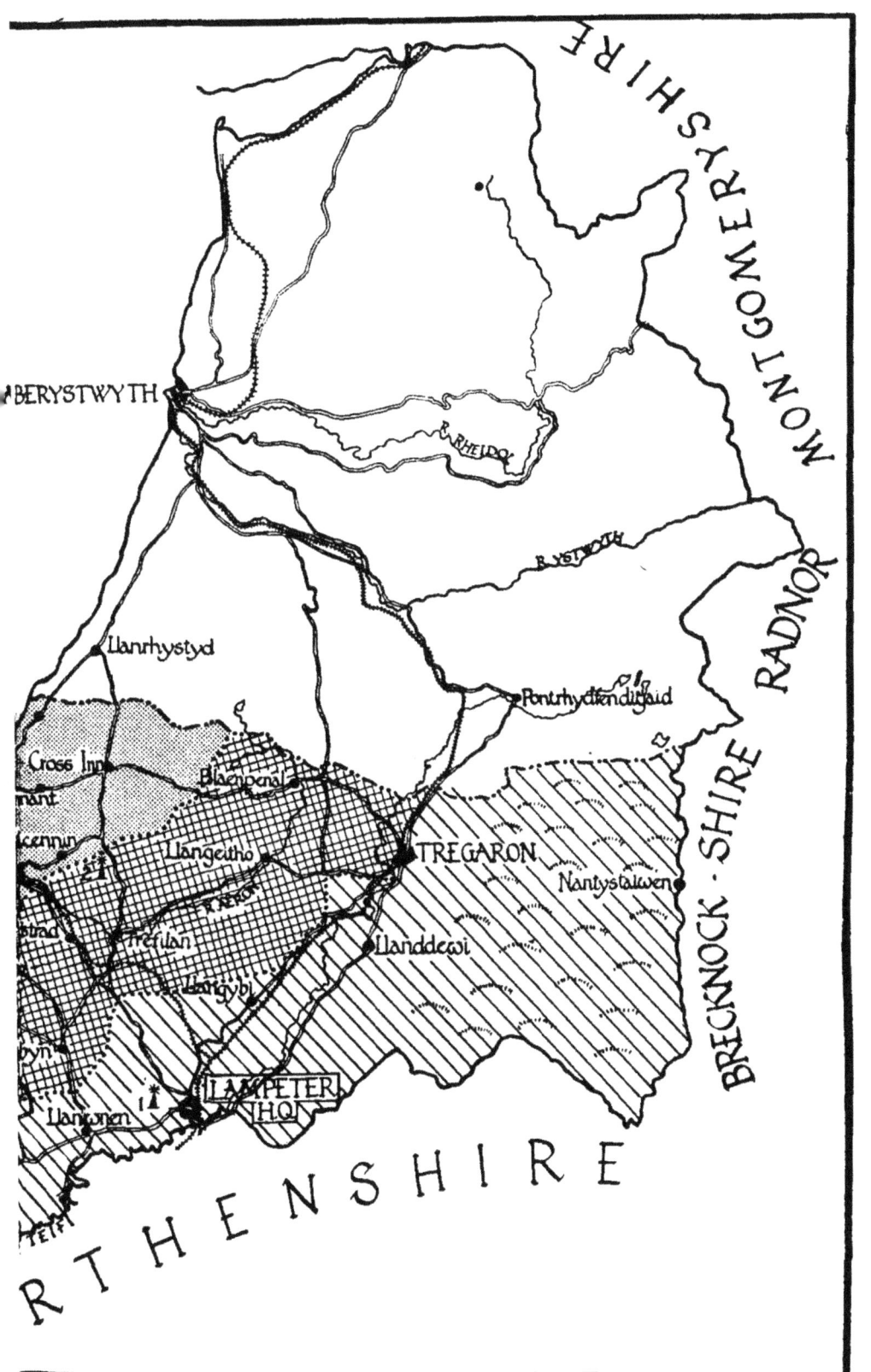

3RD CARDS. HOME GUARD

3rd CARDS. BATTALION HOME GUARD

The Naval & Military Press Ltd

Published by

The Naval & Military Press Ltd
Unit 10 Ridgewood Industrial Park,
Uckfield, East Sussex,
TN22 5QE England

Tel: +44 (0) 1825 749494
Fax: +44 (0) 1825 765701

www.naval-military-press.com
www.nmarchive.com

In reprinting in facsimile from the original, any imperfections are inevitably reproduced and the quality may fall short of modern type and cartographic standards.

THIS BOOK IS DEDICATED
TO THE OFFICERS AND MEN
OF THE 407 BATTERY R.A.,
WHO SHOWED
INCOMPARABLE VALOUR
ON MANY BATTLEFIELDS

PREFACE

IT is well that the Story of the 3rd Cards. Home Guard should be recorded. In the sweeping enemy victories of 1940 there was grave and imminent peril of invasion of this Country. These colossal events completely overshadowed the commonplace. There must be many, who would like to know what means were adopted to protect our homes against our formidable foe. This book is written to supply that information, for the sake of the present no less than the future. It does not profess to be exhaustive, but it contains references and contributions which are of local interest. The Editors feel that this handbook should not be published before the end of all hostilities, but there is also a possibility of it never appearing at all, unless done immediately on the disbandment of the HOME GUARD. Hence it was decided to put these pages together while information was still available and before the interest in the subject had been completely overshadowed by post war problem.

J. DAVIES
J. E. LLOYD   1945.

FOREWORD

IT is with very great pleasure that I agree to the request to write a foreword to this Record of the 3rd Cardiganshire Battalion Home Guard. On 14th May, 1940, Mr. Anthony Eden broadcast an appeal for volunteers for a Defence Force to protect this country from an invasion, that, following the disaster to our Armies in France, seemed a foregone conclusion. On the Sunday following the Broadcast the Lord Lieutenant (The Earl of Lisburne) summoned Sir George Fossett Roberts (Chairman T.A.A.) ; Capt. J. J. Lloyd Williams, M.C. (Chief Constable) and myself to a conference at Crosswood. The Lord Lieutenant told us that in view of the gravity of the situation His Majesty the King had called upon all Lord Lieutenants to raise a Defence Force for the protection of the country. The Lord Lieutenant stated he would himself take command of this Force in Cardiganshire and I accepted the post of Second in Command. On the following Tuesday, the Lord Lieutenant was called upon to rejoin the Welsh Guards, and the responsibility of raising the Force developed upon me. I became Zone Commander for the County with Lieut. Col. J. Albert Evans, M.C. as my Second in Command. Men came forward in large numbers and the help of those with past experience was invaluable. Over 3,000 men were enrolled by September. This Force was called " The Local Defence Volunteers "—more familiarly the " L.D.Vs." The name was later changed at the request of the Prime Minister to Home Guard.

My intention was that there should be three battalions in the County, but this was turned down by Higher Authority and only two battalions were sanctioned, one with Headquarters at Aberystwyth (1st Cards.) and one at Cardigan (2nd Cards.) under the command of Lieut. Col. D. C. Lewis and Lieut. Col. T. Evans respectively. This formation remained in operation until February, 1942, when after continuous demands the authorities acceded to my request and permission was given to form a 3rd Cards. Bn. with Headquarters at Lampeter. Lieut. Col. J. Albert Evans assumed command, his place as my second in command being taken by Lieut. Col. Ernest Evans, K.C.

On 1st February, 1943, the Officers were granted King's Commissions, the Home Guard establishment was re-organised and it was on these lines that we continued until " Stand Down " on 3rd December, 1944. I have had the honour to command the Force in

Cardiganshire from its inception until "Stand Down", first as Zone Commander and finally as Sector Commander, and it is with great satisfaction that I look back to the loyalty and zeal displayed by all ranks. May the Records of the 3rd Cards. Bn. contained in this book be an inspiration to all who read it, and may the friendships formed during our association in the Home Guard be further cemented!

B. TAYLOR LLOYD.
Colonel. Commander, Cards. Sector.

3rd CARDS. BATTALION HOME GUARD

HISTORY has a knack of repeating itself. A little juggling with dates, a change of some names, and one would think that the following events actually occurred in 1940. On the evening of the 1st December, 1796, the French Armada for Ireland anchored near Brest ready for invasion. When they did set sail, some of them reached Bantry Bay, but were unable to land any troops owing to a tremendous gale which suddenly sprang up. In this way was England saved by Divine Intervention. The French, however, were undismayed by failure and gathered together a nondescript force of galley slaves and jailbirds for a nuisance raid—the object being to stir up trouble in England and cause as much damage as possible. Their main objective apparently was Bristol, which they were detailed to burn. This accomplished, they were then to destroy docks, bridges, etc., and generally cause a state of confusion in the country around. Following on this, they were to sail to Wales, march across the mountains and threaten Chester and Liverpool. They sailed on the 17th February, 1797, and anchored off Ilfracombe where they landed a small raiding party who set fire to a farmhouse but hastily beat a retreat on hearing that the local Home Guard were on the march. Re-embarking, they crossed to the Welsh coast and landed near Fishguard, but the local Home Guard from Castle Martin, Cardigan, and Fishguard put a stop to their nefarious designs. A year later in 1798 things assumed a more serious aspect, for the enemy were known to have built in the ports of Belgium barges and flat bottomed boats, the purpose of which was obvious. Wild stories were circulated about these and other preparations for invasion. The print-shops were full of drawings of French rafts and of blood-curdling invasion posters for display on walls and church doors. These, however, had the opposite effect to what was intended and far from intimidating the people of this Country, they served a useful purpose in causing the people of Britain to harden their hearts and prepare for coming events. The Government called all able-bodied persons to arms ; thousands of volunteers were enrolled ; impassioned speeches were made in the House ; throughout the length and breadth of the country, in the towns and villages, men were to be seen drilling. So much for those days of the late eighteenth and early nineteenth century.

Let us now see how things stood in this country during the first year of the War. One well remembers people talking about a phoney or sit-down war, but they were rudely awakened when on the 9th April, 1940, Germany with startling suddenness invaded Norway and Denmark. The tempo of the War increased mightily after this. Event crowded on event. Naval actions off Norway were reported. An Expeditionary Force landed in Norway only to be withdrawn after being there less than a month. A month later on the 10th May, the Germans invaded Holland and Belgium. The British Army at the request of King Leopold moved into Belgium. Soon after, we learned of the resignation, owing to ill-health, of Mr. Neville Chamberlain. The King now invited Mr. Churchill to form a new Administration. He took up the reins of office at the time when we were in the preliminary stages of one of the greatest battles in history and so he told the House on the 13th of May he had nothing to offer but ' blood, tears and sweat.' A little later on in his speech he defined the Government policy : ' It is to wage war by sea, land and air, with all our might and with all the strength that God can give us." On the 14th of May the Dutch Army surrendered. On that fateful evening the Home Guard was born. The Secretary of State for War, Mr. Anthony Eden, announced the formation of the Local Defence Volunteers. Mr. Eden, the new Secretary of State for War, broadcasting on the evening of May 14th 1940, appealed to the country to give immediate support to the scheme to create a new force for home defence to be known as the " Local Defence Volunteers." The purpose, he indicated, would be to guard against possible landings by German parachute troops in this country.

Mr. Eden said,—" I want to speak to you tonight about the form of warfare which the Germans have been employing so extensively against Holland and Belgium—namely, the dropping of troops by parachute behind the main defensive lines. Let me say at once that the danger to us from this particular menace, although it undoubtedly exists, should not be exaggerated. We have made preparations to meet it already. Let me describe to you the system under which these parachute raids are carried out. The troops arrive by aeroplane—but let it be remembered that any such aeroplane seeking to penetrate here would have to do so in the teeth of the anti-aircraft defences of this country. If such penetration is effected, the parachutists are then dropped, it maybe by day, it may be by night. These troops are specially armed and equipped, and some of them have undergone specialised training. Their function is to seize important points, such as aerodromes, power stations, villages, railway junctions and telephone exchanges, either for the purpose of destroying them at once, or of holding them until the arrival of reinforcements. The purpose of the parachute attack is to disorganise and confuse, as a preparation for the landing of troops by aircraft. The success of such an attack depends on speed. Consequently, the measures to defeat such an attack must be prompt and rapid. It is upon this basis that our plans have been laid. You will not expect me to tell you, or the enemy, what our plans are, but we are confident that they will be effective. However, in order to leave nothing to chance and to supplement, from sources as yet untapped, the means of defence already arranged, we are going to ask you to help us, in a manner which I know will be welcome to thousands of you. Since the War began, the Government have received countless inquiries from all over the Kingdom from men of all ages who are for one reason or another not at present engaged in military service, and who wish to do something for the defence of the country. Now is your opportunity. We want large numbers of such men in Great Britain who are British subjects, between the ages of 17 and 65, to come forward now and offer their services in order to make assurance doubly sure. The name of the new force which is now to be raised will be the " Local Defence Volunteers." This name, Local Defence Volunteers, describes its duties in three words. It must be understood that this is, so to speak, a sparetime job, so there will be no need for any volunteer to abandon his present occupation. Part-time members of existing civil defence organisations should ask their officers' advice before registering under the scheme. Men who will ultimately become due for calling up under the National Service (Armed Forces) Act may join temporarily, and will be released to join the Army when they are required to serve. Now a word to those who propose to volunteer. When on duty, you will form part of the Armed Forces and your period of service will be for the duration of the war. You will not be paid but you will receive uniform and will be armed. You will be entrusted with certain vital duties, for which reasonable fitness and a knowledge of firearms are necessary. These duties will not require you to live away from your homes. In order to volunteer, what you have to do is to give in your name at your local police station ; and then as, and when we want you we will let you know. This appeal is directed chiefly to those who live in small towns, villages and less densely inhabited surburban areas. I must warn you that for certain military reasons, there will be some localities where the numbers required will be small and others where your services will not be required at all. Here then is the opportunity for which so many of you have been waiting. Your loyal help, added to the arrangements which already exist, will make and keep our country safe."

On the 19th of May, Mr. Churchill, speaking to the nation for the first time as Prime Minister, told of the tremendous battle that was then raging in France and Flanders. He ended his speech with words which were written centuries ago—"Arm yourselves, and be ye men of valour and be in readiness for the conflict."

At that stage of events surely more fitting words could not have been pronounced. Things were now rapidly working to a climax. On the 28th of May the Belgian Army surrendered. Then came the great epic of Dunkirk when from the 29th of May to the 4th of June over 300,000 men, French and British, were evacuated from the ports. It was then that Mr. Churchill made his wonderful speech in the House, ending up with—" We shall defend our island, whatever the cost may be, we shall fight on the beaches, we shall fight on the landing grounds, we shall fight in the streets, we shall fight in the hills; we shall never surrender." Finally, we read of the last episodes of the Battle of France, after which we stood alone, waiting for the whole fury and might of the enemy to be turned on us. One cannot end this short description without once more quoting Mr. Churchill's words, broadcast on the 28th June—" Let us brace ourselves to our duties, and so bear ourselves, that if the British Empire and its Commonwealth last for a thousand years, men will say, ' This was their finest hour ' ". Such was the background against which the Local Defence Volunteers were formed.

The following is a copy of a letter from the Prime Minister to all units of the Local Defence Force,—" On what may be the eve of an attempted invasion or battle for our native land, the Prime Minister desires to impress upon all persons holding responsible positions in the Government, in the Fighting Services or in the Civil Departments, their duty to maintain a spirit of alert and confident energy. While every precaustion must be taken that time and means afford, there are no grounds for supposing that more German troops can be landed in this Country, either from the air or across the sea, than can be destroyed or captured by the strong forces at present under arms. The Royal Air Force is in excellent order and at the highest strength it has yet attained. The German navy was never so weak, nor the British Army at home so strong as now. The Prime Minister expects all His Majesty's servants in high places to set an example of steadiness and resolution. They should check and rebuke expressions of loose and ill-digested opinion in their circle, or by their subordinates. They should not hesitate to report, or if necessary remove, any officers or officials who are found to be subconsciously exercising a disturbing or depressing influence and whose talk is calculated to spread alarm and despondency. Thus alone will they be worthy of the fighting men, who in the air, on the sea and on land, have already met the enemy without any sense of being outmatched in martial qualities."-[*Sgd*.) WINSTON CHURCHILL.

Immediately after Mr. Eden's appeal, there was an amazing response. Men of all ages were prepared to take up arms. They were prepared to train in the use of arms. When to the rest of the world outside this Country, all seemed lost, when our Army had left all its equipment on the beaches at Dunkirk, and when everyone was so taken up with the ordinary duties of civil life, that it was only at great personal sacrifice that sufficient time could be devoted to training, the various halls and schools throughout the Battalion area were packed with a most enthusiastic crowd learning the rudiments of foot drill and to move about as a body. The elements of military discipline were quickly accepted. Lampeter was fortunate enough through the courtesy of Mr. Oriel Morgan to procure about eighty old German rifles, which had lain peacefully at Highmead since the last War and again became useful, not for the Germans this time but for us. These old Mausers proved of great value in the feel and handling of the rifle that was soon to be supplied. As the weather improved, training was carried on out-doors and by this time those elderly and infirm men, whose willingness and eagerness proved a little too much for them, found the training interfering with their health, and gradually the various parties throughout the area consisted of sound and active men whose ages now had to be between 18 and 65. It was the endeavour of every local commander to find suitable duty for each man according to his age, ability and activity. Generally speaking, the more advanced in age took on administrative work, while the young and active took combatant service. The Ex-service men played a very important part in the training of this new civilian army ; with their past experience they were invaluable in imparting confidence and coolness into the new ranks. Their contribution to the early training can never be truly assessed. The problem of uniform had already been settled. This had to be done at the earliest opportunity so as to conform with the special marking of combatant soldiers, according to the Geneva Convention and the accepted rules of War. The first uniform—it was hardly a uniform—consisted of a khaki armband with the letters L.D.V. in black—Local Defence Volunteer. This was the first designation of the civilian army. The armband had to be worn on duty and so provided for the volunteer the privileges of the armed forces. At this stage the arms consisted of what shotguns and revolvers we possessed. Some had been handed to the police to be handed out later to volunteers. The ordinary sporting cartridge with No. 5 shot was not considered lethal enough for the purpose of defence and special cartridges with only 3 ball shot per cartridge were procured ; this apparently conformed to the legitimate use of such weapons. Training was now definitely taking shape, and soon a khaki blouse and trousers made their appearance in the ranks. The first denims arrived without caps and the first men who were fortunate enough to procure a suit hardly looked smart in khaki and trilby.

It can now be divulged that the authorities were very concerned indeed with the possibilities of an invasion of this country through Cardiganshire by the combination of the use of the sea and the high hills. Strategically, Cardiganshire owing to its sparsely populated areas was ideal as a concentration area, the roads leading from it to the industrial areas of South Wales and the Midlands presenting vast possibilities to a ruthless and determined enemy. Early in 1941, after his visit to Swansea, the Prime Minister was accompanied by the Chief of Staff on a visit to Pembrokeshire and Cardiganshire. The importance attached to the area by the War Office can best be understood perhaps, if we merely state that the Chief of Staff was in Cardiganshire on the day following his return from the Middle East.

The first official instruction issued from the Zone Commander Headquarters at Aberystwyth was as follows,—" In order that there may be some unanimity of thought regarding the functions of the L.D.V.F., especially in country districts, the following general lines should be considered—The whole principle of the force is chiefly the defence of the ' Englishman's Home,' and where there are no set observation posts it would appear that the farmer and countryman can act as a reconnoitring patrol. For instance, the farmer and neighbouring farmers have guns, are working throughout the countryside in fields, and are possibly in a position to deal at an early stage with parachutists, with a view to delaying their actions. He sends his information back from the nearest telephone to the nearest section, platoon or company headquarters, wherever they may be, for instance, a nearby village. This constitutes what might be described as the foremost line of defended localities. The information is then immediately passed through the proper channels to the Area Commander. Action taken depending on the situation would then develop on obvious lines.

B. TAYLOR LLOYD, *Zone Commander.*

The day that Wycliffe was evacuated from Stonehouse in 1939 was a fortunate one for Lampeter in more senses that one. When the L.D.V. Force was formed in May, 1940, the Staff, and boys who were of age came forward in force to offer their services on behalf of their country. It was not very long before they proved their worth, as could be seen in those early days of 1940 and 1941, before the Battalion was formed, when they took a very active part in the various exercises up and down the County of Cardigan. When they formed a part of " C " Company of the 1st. Battalion which up to 1942 covered a vast area, the Section went even as far afield as the mountains near Devil's Bridge—a veritable Sabbath Day's journey indeed. On this occasion the enemy was provided by the students of Aberystwyth University and one can well remember the friendly arguments that ensued after the " show " was over as to whether the defenders or the enemy had been seen. Such statements as, ' I saw you crossing the ridge,' or ' You went across that gap like a lot of sheep,' were frequently heard. This, of course, was in the days

before anybody had been initiated into the mysteries of Battle Drill so that the various ways of propelling oneself along the ground were unknown. It was not till later on, that one used cover as a means to an end, i.e., that of destroying the enemy. Another exercise in which the Section took part was one which had the merits of being on a somewhat larger scale, involving the employment of a considerable number of umpires. The scene of action was Aberayron and its approaches. The enemy had landed on the beaches. Parachutists had been dropped in the neighbourhood of Hengeraint Wood to harass, and, if possible to prevent any reinforecements from coming in from Lampeter to succour the beleagured garrison. The Wycliffe Section had a definite task to do, namely to 'winkle' out these parachutists from the positions they held on the high ground above the road. This they did successfully after suffering some casualties, some of which they had incurred, so at least, they were informed by an Umpire, through firing on their own men. However, ' all's well that ends well ' and they marched in triumph to Aberayron, but their triumph was short-lived for as they approached the part of the road where it turns into the town itself, they were met by withering M.G. fire. Not to be outdone by this new turn of events, the Section immediately debouched and dealt with the situation, compelling the Enemy to surrender in a very short space of time. Early in 1941 the Section took part in an exercise in which they acted as the ' Enemy,' having been dropped in the area round Olwen. Their main objective was the railway station at Lampeter. One of their number had worked his way earlier on to a point in the wood on Llettytwppa from where he could observe what was going on, in, and around the Station and report to his confederates who were worming their wet and slimy way through the woods between Olwen and Llettytwppa. Unfortunately for him, however, he was unable to pass on any information. Whilst moving to a better view point he unwittingly disturbed some sheep. The movement of these sheep, in addition to an increased cawing of crows, was spotted by some hawkeyed observers posted near the station. From that movement the doom of the ' Spy ' was sealed. He endeavoured to work his way back in the direction from which his pals were approaching, but he was soon rounded up, taken down to the post, questioned and afterwards led through the town to H.Q. like Caractacus in the days of old. The other parachutists, having to work blindly, were rounded up in due course. From this exercise the useful lesson of ' avoid all animals ' was learned.

In these early days, and indeed later on, Llettytwppa was a favourite training ground, lending itself naturally for such a purpose in that it contains a fairly large quarry where one could practice to become a marksman with a .22 rifle, or to throw live grenades.

As a matter of fact every man had to throw two before he was entitled to wear a Proficiency Badge. When the 3rd Battalion was formed in 1942, the Wycliffe Section came under the wing of " C " Company of that Battalion, acting as a Mobile Section. Later on, when the Battle Platoon was formed, some of the Section became members of that famous detachment and acquitted themselves well. In a short time, however, the Section ceased to exist as a separate Section, its numbers being somewhat depleted owing to the fact that the numbers of boys eligible for the Home Guard decreased to such an extent that it was decided to absorb the few that remained into the Company. Finally, only the members of the Staff were left and they became Officers either at Bn. Head Quarters or in the Company filling in posts of Transport, Signals, and Intelligence Officers, Officer Commanding "C" Company, second in Command "C" Company and Officer Commanding No. 1 Platoon.

The ringing of Church Bells seemed a simple and effective form of giving the alarm and up to the very end this became a hardy annual at all conferences and meetings of the Home Guard. A satisfactory method of signifying immediate danger in an area was only evolved after considerable discussion and trial. Difficulties and misunderstandings had to be continually dealt with. The presence of any enemy parties seen in a neighbourhood was to be notified to the nearest Home Guard, who would confirm the incident. He would then proceed to the nearest church and order the bells to be tolled by the bell ringer. Under no circumstances were other bells to take up the alarm. In certain areas the rule was not adhered to, with the result that vast areas were put in a state of unnecessary alarm. Access to the church bell was often a difficulty which had to be considered. On the whole, this system of raising the alarm was considered quite satisfactory and the church bells throughout the land were silent for nearly three years until the risk of invasion by sea or by air was considered negligible. Early in 1943 the homely and friendly ringing was once more heard and it was a great relief to have back again a familiar custom which appeared so commonplace before the War. The calling out of the Home Guard in a rural area still presented difficulties. In times of danger the whole area was in a state of expectation and news travelled with amazing rapidity. As in the Bush with its drum beating, there was no tangible form of alarm, but an indefinable system of Bush telephony seemed to work satisfactorily; even better than any of the defined forms of alarm.

As stated above, the church bells were silent for a period of nearly three years but in April 1943 an order was issued legalising the ringing of the bells for service held on Sundays and other Holy Days. The following incident proved the value of the early order forbidding the use of Church Bells except as a means of giving the alarm. When the famous attack on Lampeter by American troops took place in November, 1943, the captain of one of the mobile units conceived the idea of executing a flank attack on the right of our position by working his way round by Llanwnen, Maestir, etc. On reaching one of these places he was astonished to hear the church bell ringing. Not knowing that the original order with respect to the ringing of church bells had been rescinded, and assuming that the ringing of this particular bell was a signal to the Home Guard troops that the invading forces were near, he immediately gave an order that the sexton or whoever was responsible for the ringing of the bell, should be taken out from the belfry and held until the troops were well on their way. One can imagine the amazement of the sexton when he was confronted by some soldiers with fixed bayonets who yanked him out unceremoniously, despite his vigorous protestations that he was ringing the bell for a church service. Having no one to appeal to, the American officer assumed that he had acted correctly. This incident, however, has an exciting sequel. When the self-same American officer was taking part in a somewhat more serious battle—to wit, Runstedt's break through towards the Maas, he found himself almost alone in a certain small town, with the enemy practically outflanking his positions. Whilst he was considering what he should do—and his position was an unenviable one—he suddenly heard the ringing of a church bell. At once his thoughts went back to that very wet day when he last heard a church bell rung in the vicinity of Lampeter. Being a man used to making quick decisions he gave swift orders to some of his men to stop the ringing of the bell and slay the sexton. His men soon discovered the church, mounted up to the belfry, shot the sexton, who was actually a German spy, and prevented the bell from being used on future occasions for the giving of signals to the enemy. Thus did the Home Guard unconsciously play their part in defeating and upsetting the plans of the enemy.

Another system of indicating the approach of enemy aircraft was by means of sirens. These were installed in the summer of 1940 at Lampeter and Aberayron and the sound of the siren became a very familiar one. A warbling or wailing note for one minute indicated raiding aircraft in the vicinity and a continuous note for one minute indicated raiders past or what became more generally known as the 'all clear.' The control of the siren was under the direction of the police who acted on the receipt of yellow, purple and red warnings. The yellow warning indicated enemy aircraft in the neighbourhood, the purple warning indicated enemy aircraft in the immediate vicinity and the red warning, raiders overhead, while the white indicated 'All clear.' The siren sounded only on the receipt of the red and white warnings. All organisations received these warnings by telephone and acted accordingly. During the bombing of

Cardiff, Swansea and Liverpool the wailing of the siren became familiar and commonplace, and as war supplanted peace so sirens supplanted bells.

In 1942, Professor Harris took over the control of the St. David's College Home Guard and secured an issue of clothing. All were sorry to lose the civilian atmosphere of training under Sgt. Cadman and were sorrier still after the first route march in new boots. A number of men hobbled to College Chapel next morning, (in fact, nearly all College). Training started in earnest with probably the largest unit of young fit men in the Battalion. Training for rugby was a help as well, and so gradually reduced the time taken to march round Falcondale. At this time there were about 90, organised into three sections, under Lieut. Harris as Platoon Officer with Sgt. D. H. Price as Platoon Sergeant. .22 rifles were issued and many afternoons were spent shooting in the Old Quarry, much to Prof. Harris' chagrin at the sight of the first targets, but afterwards to his delight. By the end of the Easter term, St. David's made up a well trained unit organised and ready for any squalls which might blow up. A climax of the term's training came when orders were issued that there would be an emergency call-out on two occasions at some date during the week. All were eating dinner comfortably at Mrs. Butler's, when Cpl. Dennis put his head in the room and shouted ' Emergency. Muster in 20 minutes.' Such was the hurry to obey that all got up and left their dinners. All mustered at the College School and were very disappointed when nothing special happened. However, the reward came the second time there was a call-out, by having a chance to fight against some of the country platoons. An amusing incident occurred when Major Parrott and his Platoon Sergeant, after having crept across Harford Square in stockinged feet, threw a bomb into 10, Bridge Street thinking it full of the enemy, only to find that a very gallant Section under Cpl. Herbert were smoking and relaxing after a very well executed and successful attack. In conclusion, it speaks well for the training received if one fact is noted, i.e. that of the 30 or 40 men who left to join the forces and continue the fight in real earnest nearly all were commissioned in some regiment or other of the Army.

Perhaps an Intelligence Officer stands to get his leg pulled and to have good humoured shafts hurled at him more than anybody else. The very word ' Intelligence ' simply asks for it. Be that as it may, the work is extremely interesting and covers a wide field. An Intelligence Officer has to be a sort of walking encyclopaedia ; he is the Commanding Officer's right hand man ; he has to hold himself in readiness to take on the Adjutant's job ; he must be prepared, if necessary, to take on even the onerous and thankless job of Battalion Quartermaster. So much for the Intelligence Officer. The first stage of Intelligence Training in the Battalion consisted in getting the men, as a whole, security minded. In those early days of the Battalion in 1942, things were not going too well, for propoganda played a big part. Rumours were spread abroad, and, unfortunately, too many people listened to them. It is a strange quality possessed by many of us that we like to pose before our neighbours as tellers of tidings, good or bad. The more lurid the story, the more we go up in the estimation of our listeners. Thus it became the duty of the Intelligence Officer to persuade the men in the Battalion that " He that keepeth his mouth keepeth his life ; but he that openeth wide his lips shall have destruction ". In this he was aided by some excellent films, one of the best of which was ' Next of Kin.' One often wonders whether, if the Germans had had the temerity to land in this country, there were many persons who would have acted as Fifth Columnists and given their valuable assistance to the enemy. Fortunately we never had the chance of discovering this. No doubt there were many people who acted ' in a suspicious way,' probably more through curiosity than anything else. We were not troubled much by such folk, but there were one or two scares, which, of course, came to nothing, but one is worth recording : One day, the I.O. was approached by a certain gentleman—who shall be nameless—who informed him that he had noticed a man behaving suspiciously ; in fact he had been going around trying to borrow a bicycle, and in addition, he had been asking leading questions about a certain prohibited area situated not so very far away. Apparently, this man was successful in his search for a bicycle, and rode off to the place about which he was so curious. What became of him was never found out despite the most exhaustive enquiries. Perhaps he never existed and was only a figment of imagination on the part of somebody who wished to pose as the teller of a good story. Anyhow, such incidents helped to keep one on the 'qui vive.'

When the Intelligence Sections in Battalion and Companies had been formed, the work became more varied. One of the essential parts of a man's training in the Intelligence Section is map reading at which he must become proficient. And it must be remarked here that despite the fact that there was a shortage of maps, the men in the Home Guard and Company Sections aquitted themselves well in the Proficiency Tests in which Map reading was a compulsory subject. It has been stated earlier on that an I.O. had to be a sort of walking encyclopaedia. The men, also, had to possess a wide knowledge of such things as appertained to the whereabouts of military units in the Area : the situation of all H.G. Units in the Battalion area and their telephone numbers, the various H.G. Commands from District downwards, everything to do with the Civil Defence Services, and other things too numerous to mention. All these facts had to be tabulated by the respective I.Os. in what were called Location Lists. These, of course, would have proved of great value to any Regular Army Units, who might have had to fight in the Battalion area. Then the men had to be initiated into the mysteries of message writing. How many were the 'raspberries' received from the 'higher-ups' because it was thought that the men, and, may it be said, the Officers, too, were not proficient enough in this mysterious art. However, experience teaches, and before the end a high state of proficiency had been reached. As a matter of fact, the Army message form, which rejoiced in the title of A.F.C. 2136, presented a number of pitfalls to the unwary. To the unfortunate being who suffered from a poor memory it was the source of a good deal of trouble. Did one put SOUTH or S? or again, S.W. or SOUTH-WEST? When did one use capital letters, etc.? Of course, all messages were not written. Some had to be sent by word of mouth. Practice in this always afforded great amusement. Somehow or other, the original message rarely got to its destination without undergoing a twisting which would be thought to be impossible. When the time-honoured joke about the officer who sent an urgent message back to H.Q. for reinforcements was told, the audience laughed politely as if to say: 'Try it on us, we would never make the mistake of saying, 'send 3-4; am going to a dance' instead of 'send reinforcements, am going to advance.' But they did it again and again! As has been stated earlier, Intelligence covers a wide field. It was very necessary for the section to know as much as possible about the enemy against whom we were fighting, so lectures on the German Army always proved popular. Lastly a man had to be taught to be observant, to notice the smallest details, and to be able to send in a concise report on what he had seen. The work in an Intelligence Section was always interesting, especially during exercises when the quick passing back of information was vital, the keeping of logs essential, and the ability to read a map well, invaluable. Various exercises were held throughout the area to test intercommunications, etc., during which the services of the Civil Defence and even Civilians were called upon. These proved of extreme value and interest. Everybody played his or her part with zest, and the exercise was always made as realistic as possible. American troops, when available, were only too ready to give their valuable assistance and act as the 'enemy.' Civilians were 'dropped' in various spots as enemy agents, often carrying with them false identification papers, some of which had been so cleverly faked as to deceive even the most observant. Much praise is due to these hardy people who took part in these exercises in all sorts of weather. Why was it that, when an exercise was due to take place, it invariably rained?

Although Proficiency Tests do not come under the province of Intelligence, it fell to the lot of the men in the I.S. to assist their brethren who were not fortunate enough to receive specialised training in various subjects. After all, the Intelligence men were carriers of information, so their training acted in a two-fold way. Whilst one is on the subject of Proficiency Tests, it must be realised that, as in any other kind of Exam., oral or written, many amusing answers were given to questions. For instance, Sector Command changed hands many times ; a Company Commander was elevated to the rank of Colonel more than once ; the name of a certain Medical Officer was remembered by the fact that hissname coincided with a certain beverage ! One Home Guard provided an amusing interlude during the Test on Battlecraft, which, of course, was carried on out of doors. The men were being tested on the choosing of suitable fire positions after having been duly warned that ' Cover from View ' does not necessarily mean ' Cover from fire ' ! When the squad had taken up their positions, it was discovered that one of their number was missing. He was eventually discovered well and truly hidden like Moses in the bullrushes in a large furze bush, firing with a total disregard of direction. It must be added, however, that this particular H.G., having profited by his mistakes, is now the proud possessor of a Proficiency Certificate. It is not possible to conclude this brief account without making reference to the Officers who acted as I.Os. during the years in which the Battalion functioned :—" A " Company—Lt. Marter and Lt. Parry ; " B " Company—Lt. E. Jones and Lt. Jones Evans ; " C " Company—Lt. Rees, Lt. Rogers and Lt. George ; " D " Company—Lt. D. Thomas. Nor must we forget the men who in all conditions of weather often travelled distances which in themselves would have provided a legitimate excuse for non-attendance. What, one may ask, has been the outcome of all this training ? One thing is certain the men derived benefit from their training, they were ready for any task that might be imposed upon them, and, above all, a spirit of good comradeship was formed, without which nothing can be achieved. And finally it was the duty of ' Intelligence ' to instruct every man in the Battalion in giving simple orders in German and a list of useful phrases was supplied.

Halt ! Who goes there ? *Halt, wer da* ? (*Halt vair dar*) ?
Come closer. *Kommt hierher*. (*Commt hearhair*).
Surrender. *Ergebt euch* (plural). (*Airgabt oych*) *Ergieb dich* (singular), (*Airgeeb dich*).
Do not shoot. *Nicht schiessen*. (*Nicht sheesen*).
Throw down your arms. *Waffen wegwerfen*. (*Vaffen veckvairfen*).
Stand still. *Bleib stehen*. (*Blibe shtayen*).
Go in front of me. *Vorausgehen*. (*Forow-sgayen*).
Forward. *Vorwarts*. (*Forvairts*).
At once. *Sofort*. (*Sofort*).

Double.   *Marsch, marsch.*   (*Marsh, marsh*).
Faster.   *Schneller.*   (*Schneller*).
Slower.   *Langsam.*   (*Langsam*).
Left.   *Links.*   (*Links*).
Right.   *Rechts.*   (*Rechts*).
Stop.   *Halt.*   (*Hallt*).
Come back.   *Kommt Zuruch.*   (*Kommt tsooreck*).

Upon the formation of the Battalion active and progressive steps were immediately taken to form a close liaison between the Home Guard and the Civil Defence Services in the Battalion Area. With the continual changes in the military situation and the unceasing thought given to possible steps that might be taken by the enemy— a state of affairs really serious and urgent during those years— although perhaps difficult to place in their proper setting when looked at from the view point of the present, it became a matter of prime importance to keep in continuous touch with these services. Incidents in or affecting the area, caused by the enemy would be reported through the A.R.P. Control Centre with Prof. D. Dawson in charge as Sub-Controller, whose territory more or less coincided with the Battalion area. For A.R.P. purposes there were three divisions corresponding roughly with the old areas of the Lampeter, Aberayron and Tregaron Rural District Councils. Serving under the Sub-Controller in each of these areas were :—Lampeter—Mr. G. Quan, A.R.P.S. Aberayron—Mr. E. J. Thomas, A.R.P.S., and Tregaron—Lieut. Ezer Evans, A.R.P.S. In addition there were wardens in all districts, First Aid Parties and Ambulances with these additional facilities at Lampeter : one Mobile Ambulance Unit under Dr. W. R. Bowen ; Red Cross Detachments under Dr. E. Evans, M.C.; Decontamination Squad under Mr. H. H. Thomas ; and Rescue Parties under Mr. D. S. Harries. Reciprocal arrangements were made for lectures by the A.R.P. on Gas, the treatment of and identification of the most common gases, anti-personnel bombs, H.E. Bombs and Gas Bombs ; and by the Home Guard, on weapons and grenades. During the whole of that anxious period the A.R.P. and Home Guard worked 'hand in glove.' From time to time exercises were arranged by the Sub-Controller involving all the services and in the resulting 'inquests' it was noticeable there was more praise than kicks given to those taking part. Between brackets, as it were, it can now be revealed that the imagination of the Sub-Controller at times was such that those taking part were set some pretty problems.

Battalion Head Quarters drew out a scheme showing precisely what aid it could give the A.R.P. if and when involved, and details were available at Head Quarters from all centres in its area through the four Invasion Committees of what kind of help was required.

Each Military Commander knew exactly whom to send, where he was to be sent to, what his duties were and under what circumstancs, he could be spared from Home Guard duties.

Contact was also kept with the Police through Inspector T. O. Price and with the Special Constables through Superintendent A. W. Davies and Inspector D. R. Thomas, and if not themselves, the Home Guard undertook to provide help in keeping order, controlling traffic, etc., in the event of a heavy raid. The N.F.S. under Column Officer F. Smith were given the same assurances and there were instances in the Battalion area where the Home Guard were called upon to help in controlling and putting our fires. All the Royal Observer Corps posts were visited and in addition to arrangements for mutual information the R.O.C. post personnel were given facilities to get their firing practices on H.G. ranges under H.G. supervision and guidance. Subject to certain conditions the R.O.C. would transmit messages affecting the H.G. On the coasts, coast-watchers were assured of help from the local companies and in certain districts the coast-guards were given facilities to withdraw to other posts if and when their own became untenable. The state of preparedness attained by the Battalion was mainly due to this ready co-operation, and without giving unnecessary details it can be said that not once did any Section, Platoon, Company or the Battalion stage an exercise without the ready help of the A.R.P., Police, Special Constables, R.O.C., and N.F.S. On the coast the same applied to the Coast-guard and Coast Watchers. In addition to the two other battalions in Cardiganshire, the 1st Battalion to the North and the 2nd to the South, we had common boundaries with the 4th and 5th Carms. and the 2nd Brecs. In the 'no man's land' part of our area between Tregaron and the River Towy in its upper reaches, there was a mounted patrol under Mr. Thomas Jones, Nantllwyd who had contact with our Battalion at Tregaron. Contact was also kept with the 4th Carms. at Rhandirmwyn and with the 2nd Brecons at Nantstalwyn. No praise is too high for these mounted hawk-eyed scouts, and at all times Battalion was perfectly confident that no incident of a suspicious nature could take place in this sparsely populated area without its being seen and reported.

The Mounted Patrol was unique in the Home Guard organisation and consisted of about a dozen shepherds mounted on their little mountain ponies. Each man was always accompanied by a couple of sagacious sheep dogs and their 'beat' covered a large tract of hilly land, thinly populated and probably the wildest and most desolate area in Britain. This area consisted of portions of five Counties, i.e., Cardiganshire, Breconshire, Carmarthenshire, Merionethshire and Radnorshire. Liaison was established with these Counties and the privilege of patrolling this vast area fell to the Mounted Shepherds of North East Cardiganshire. Both in temperament and ability this small guerilla band probably constituted the most fearsome and daring of any in the country. They attended no parades owing to the fact that their farms were so widely separated, but it is on record that they attended one parade on the last day—the final 'Stand Down' parade at Lampeter. They had looked forward to this no less than the rest of the Battalion who only knew of them in a hush hush fashion. They duly arrived at their rendezvous in the hills and were carried the twenty miles to Lampeter in a large cattle lorry—men and ponies together. Their appearance in the final parade created quite a sensation as most men were quite ignorant of their existence.

The Regular Training Staff made its appearance about the middle of 1942, and concentrated its efforts on bringing Home Guard training up to date. The state of training at this juncture was found to be varied in character, but the keenness of every one was unmistakeable. One found a stiffenning of '·old sweats' from the last War, many of whom had won fame in glorious exploits. They did remarkably good work in the L.D.V. days and afterwards in getting the men together, training them at a time when equipment was a minus quantity and ammunition non-existent. Then the active, virile young men also joined the ranks, in many cases men who were debarred from joining the Regular Army on account of employment of national importance. It was a very good thing to have this mixture of experience and youth. In a rural area, such as that of the 3rd Battalion, one found many, who were well versed in the craftiness of the 'poacher' and at the same time understood the wiliness of the 'water bailiff'; the cunning power of the 'hunter' as well as the dexterity of the 'hunted' were qualities ever present. Who could fail under such circumstances, whether strategy called for 'Attack' or 'Defence.' With such material to handle, success was assured.

The Home Guard took to the Regular Staff right from the beginning and perfect harmony existed all along. Officers and other ranks showed a willingness to attend courses at the various Company areas, and Travelling Wings visited the area from time to time, bringing with them the latest information from the various theatres of war. Praise is due to the Captain Quartermaster for the way he tackled the job of Quartermaster and Adjutant for quite a time until the Regular Adjutant came along. When the team was complete, the Quartermaster was able to attend to the 'Q' side, whilst the Adjutant and Permanent Staff Instructors concentrated on training. Looking back one remembers an exercise in September 1942 held at Maestir—one which may now be referred to as the Battle of Maestir. The morning reminded one very strongly of that grey misty morning in March 1918.

Major Thornton was the principal actor on that day and with his usual skill and assiduity nobly carried out his task. The important Lessons of ' Correct Information,' ' Contact,' ' Control,' ' Keeping Touch,' were well brought out and formed a basis for future training.

The Wyclifie College Officers and Contingent became a valuable asset to the ' Third ' as time went on, and the Battalion benefited greatly from the many excellent demonstrations put on by Major Parrott. This Battalion also put in some good work in the Sector Battle Platoon Exercise and made good use of that Special Platoon for demonstration afterwards. The Home Guardsman soon showed his prowess with his personal weapons, but was rather perplexed when different types of new weapons began to appear at odd times, thereby necessitating a change of tactics in training. With the many lessons brought to light from the various Theatres of War and the rapid changes in the progress of the War, it became apparent that changes in the mode of Home Guard training would have to be introduced. With the limited time for training the Home Guard were to be sympathised with and complimented upon the way they competed with the various issues put before them. What a headache was caused by the change of nomenclature— Tank traps, Defended Localities, Anti-Tank Islands, Islands of Resistance, Centres of Resistance—Do THEY remember them? ' Know your own ground ' was an ever present slogan and did they know it? Ask the boys of Pennant and Cross Inn and many other country places when you watched them on Night Patrols. Major Talvan Davies and the Regular Training Officer were tricked more than once.

One remembers the exercises in the Ceibach area, when the slickness of Q.S.M. Parry had to be watched by the C.O., Major Phillips and Col. Jarvis Jones, the Regular Training Officer. Well do we remember those Sunday afternoons. One must refer to the splendid co-operation that existed between the ' Third ' and the U.S. Forces training in the area. Several useful exercises were carried out together and one large ambitious exercise was held on that memorable wet Sunday in November 1943. What a day! The Home Guard did their work admirably on that occasion. One must not forget the value gained by the Home Guard individually and collectively from the Proficiency Tests so well run by this Battalion. Above all the ' esprit de corps ' was excellent, many old friendships were cemented closer, many new friends were made and it is hoped that this true spirit of camaraderie has continued in some form or other in the days of peace, when this noble country of ours will need that same spirit of co-operation to meet its post war problems.

Finally, a word of praise for the part played by the women folk at home in helping their menfolk to attend parades. It is rumoured that Mrs. ' Rhywun ' Morgan told her neighbour that John, her husband, was a much better man since he joined the Home Guard. He had become more docile in his demeanour, having lost that spirit of aggresiveness (probably on parade or on the assault course) ; in fact he was so docile in spirit that, to her amazement, all she had to say now was ' FOLLOW ME ' and he did so like a lamb. Had Mrs. Morgan been evesdropping when some enthusiastic Squad Leader had been out on exercise, or did Cpl. John Morgan talk in his sleep ? Tell it not in Felinfach ! or was it Gath !

Although Proficiency Tests became general and compulsory in 1943, this Battalion held a test of proficiency for information purposes in June 1942. It was purely and simply a Battalion examination in order to find out the standard reached in each of the four companies in Map Reading, the 36 Grenade, Musketry (Theory) and Musketry (Practical), Aiming and Trigger pressing. The requisite questions were drawn out at one of the Battalion Conferences and the personnel in each Company examined by the Company Commander and Company Officers.

Later in 1942 an Army Council Instruction appeared, giving all Battalions lines along which tests of proficiency were to be carried out. Successful candidates in this 'official' test were entitled to wear a diamond shaped piece of red cloth on the right sleeve of the Battle Dress, each edge to measure one inch. In addition men found proficient were excused certain hours parades each month. The subjects of this test were divided into two parts. Part I was made up of General Knowledge, 36 M. Grenade, Rifle (Theory), Rifle (Practical), and Part II First Aid, Gas and Map Reading. Company Commanders made arrangements for target shooting with .22 and .300 in their own areas. Lieuts. J. Davies, J. E. Lloyd and H. A. Harries, were appointed at a Battalion conference as an examination board whose duty it was to draw out the necessary questions and appoint examiners to attend each Company Head Quarters in turn to carry out the examination. The numbers presenting themselves for those tests speaks volumes for the enthusiasm of the members and for the excellent team work between Company Commanders, their Officers, N.C.O's. and men. The first Company to be examined in Part I. was 'B' Company at Felinfach in January 1943 and it is only just to state, that at this preliminary effort the Board learned more than anyone else. There were 31 men anxious to show their knowledge of Musketry (Theory) Aiming, Trigger pressing, Snap Shooting and Rapid Firing, General Knowledge and First Aid. In its ignorance the Board had appointed one examiner for each subject. A long queue waiting to be examined was enough to daunt the most stouthearted, but with some patience and a great deal of sweat each man was duly examined. To gain the proficiency badge the Battalion had decided on the somewhat high standard of 60% in all subjects plus either an 8" group with the .300 Rifle at 100 yards or a 2" group with .22 Rifle at 25 yards. The next Company to be examined was 'A' Company when 59 men were examined in record time, the Board having appointed a sufficient number of examiners. 'D' Company presented 26 men and 'C' Company 128, making a total of 242 candidates. Part II subjects were Map Reading, Gas and the No. 36 M. Grenade, arrangements having been made for target shooting by each Company Commander.

The final results were rather disappointing owing in most cases to lack of shooting practice. In all subjects the total gaining their Proficiency Badge was 78. Visitors from Sector and Sub-District were present at each of these tests and were unanimous in their praise of the organisation and methods of carrying on the examination. Some outside Battalions were even advised to get into touch with the 3rd Cards. before commencing their own Proficiency Tests which made Battalion H.Q. and the Examination Board justly proud.

Two invaluable lessons were learnt in the Proficiency badge tests, one that the badge had to be won only by hard work and application and, two, the Battalion Commander and the Company Commanders found where the weaknesses were, thus giving them a sound idea where to concentrate on training. In May 1943 further instructions were issued giving the qualifications for, and conditions governing the award of the Home Guard Proficiency Badge and Certificates. In addition to authority to wear a badge as laid down in the A.C.I. already referred to in January 1943 those already qualified under the old conditions could sit this further test and on requalifying were entitled to wear a bar, consisting of a strip of red cloth one inch by one quarter of an inch, horizontally below the lowest point of the Proficiency badge. In addition to the award of a badge those qualifying under these new conditions were entitled to a proficiency certificate. This new Certificate was a form of record of a man's attainments and upon its production by those joining the Royal Navy, Army or the Royal Air Force, the Officer Commanding would immediately know the proficiency reached by the holder. In this way the Home Guard not only made themselves proficient but saved a great deal of time to the Services. The objects of awarding badges and certificates were therefore : to encourage all members to reach a high standard of training and to be recognised as proficient by the wearing of a badge ; to give the standard to be reached before any 'easing-up' of training was allowed ; and thirdly to give to the proficient members of the Home Guard a certificate of proficiency which was of value to those joining the Royal Navy, the Army or the Royal Air Force. The Examination Board decided to divide this test into three parts : (1) General knowledge, Musketry and the 36 M. Grenade ; (ii) Lewis Gun, Browning, M.M.G., Sten,

Northover Projector, Spigot Mortar, 3" O.S.B. Gun, Signalling ; (iii) Map reading and First Aid to include Gas. There was in addition a test in Battle Craft plus Range work either with .300 Rifle or .22 Rifle an 8" group at 100 yards with .300, or 2" group at 25 yeards with .22 rifle. To gain his certificate a candidate had to satisfy the examiner in Part I, all subjects. Part II, one subject plus one subject from Part III and Battlecraft. In General Knowledge suitable questions were drawn out by the Board, four out of five of which had to be answered correctly. In Musketry or the Rifle, the following tests had to be passed—Aiming, Aiming off, rapid fire fire and firing positions. 36 Grenade. All Candidates must show a sound knowledge of the methods of priming and throwing the No. 36 M. Grenade and must have thrown not less than two live grenades. As can be seen, these tests were rather exacting and particularly so when one remembers that all members of the H.G. had their civilian work to do. To give a clear idea of what was expected from the candidates we submit these questions which were actually asked in Part I of the 1943 tests :—

General Knowledge. State the position of two telephones in your area? Give the telephone number of the Coy. HQ or Platoon HQ or Bn. HQ? Where is the nearest Railway Station? Police Station? Name the person in charge? The nearest First Aid Post? Nearest Doctor? Where is your nearest A.R.P. Post? The nearest Fire Station? State what you would do if a bomb was dropped in your area? Name your Battalion Commander ; Company Commander ; Platoon Commander ; Section Commander? Name one other Battalion Officer? Name the Regiment to which we are attached? Name the Military Units in the Battalion area? What would you do on Mustering?

Rifle Theory. How far in front of a man who is walking across your front 300 yards away should you aim? If at the double? With a right to left wind how much should you aim off at (*a*) 100 yards? (*b*) 300 yards? Aim is taken at an aiming disc in the prone position and four shots taken. Three good shots must be made out of four ; A man on the Command ' Rapid ' comes into the aim (lying position) at the aiming disc. On the word ' fire ' he will fire five shots in one minute without removing the rifle from the shoulder. Four shots should be fired correctly. The examiner will check the aim with the aiming disc.

No. 36 M. Grenade. What are the first safety precautions before handling any Grenades? State the colour of live grenades? How do you recognise the two types of fuses in use in igniter sets? State the colours of both fuses and time of burning? What do you do with the safety pin after withdrawing it from the grenade? Describe the main parts of the grenade? Why is high throwing essential?

What happens when a No. 36 M. Grenade explodes? What is inserted into the Grenade before it becomes primed? How do you distinguish 'live' grenades? Explain the method of priming? Explain the mechanism which causes the striker to ignite the fuse.

In Part II the subjects chosen were Map Reading and First Aid (including Gas). The questions set were as follows :—

Map Reading. Two maps of different scales are provided and two points or places chosen on each, the candidate has to find the distance between them using the scales ; A point is chosen on a map and the candidate is expected to—Give the height, the nature of the ground where the contours are close together, the nature of the ground where the contours are a good distance apart? Given the Map Reference find the spot? Given a point, give the map reference? Five conventional signs are shown and candidates are expected to know their meanings? Give three methods of finding the North?

First Aid. This is a First Field dressing—What does the package consist of? Demonstrate to me how you would apply it? How do you deal with shock or collapse? What do you mean by a tourniquet? How do you improvise a tourniquet? What are the dangers attached to applying a tourniquet? How would you treat a case of external haemorrhage? (Priority of treatment and priority of transport)—You have come across two casualties, one a case of internal haemorrhage and the other a case of torn off limb—State which should have priority of treatment and why? Mention one or two conditions which should have priority of transport? Where is the nearest Regimental Aid Post? Without the aid of stretchers tell me how you would carry a casualty a short distance?

Fieldcraft. 1. Movement by day under observation—Sections of 10 were asked to move along the road for a distance of 300 yards or so under partial observation by the enemy from an O.P. Men being sent off singly at about minute intervals. Judges watched for —Position of Arms and Methods of advancing. 2. Choosing firing positions. Men spaced out in a line five yards apart and after advancing a little were ordered to take up firing positions. Judges examined cover and looked for these points—Ability to see target ; Free use of weapons ; Over or around cover. 3. Crawling under fire— at least three crawls were necessary, stomach, cossack and monkey crawl. 4. Camouflage against background (two judges)—one judge stays with men to see that all take part. The other walks away a distance of 150 yards or so, and turns round and observes after receiving a signal that men are ready. He then orders No. 1 move, etc., giving in his report the number seen. Men may not conceal themselves higher than their waist behind cover but may garnish their persons with the natural flora. 5. Preparation for and Movement by Night—Men given a few minutes for preparation. Points for

Judge—Removal of tin hats ; Blackened faces ; Tie up swivels ; Noisy equipment ; Remove from their persons any documents which might be of use to the enemy. Men were then given an objective about 150 yards away and told to imagine it is a fairly dark night, that they have to get within grenade range of it and go through the actions of throwing a grenade. Points for judges—Method of walking ; Direction of advance (avoidance of long grass or rushes) ; Periodical pauses to listen ; Keep low to get observation and avoid the skyline ; Direction of wind or any continuous noise taken advantage of ; Whether the grenade is thrown from cover or in the open. 6. Reaction to being under heavy fire—Men will be advanced in line at about 5 yards intervals and will suddenly be told they are under heavy fire—Judge will note the individual reaction.

The examination for proficiency badge and certificate was commenced in December 1943 and the three parts including the Battlecraft were completed in the early months of 1944. In all, 319 Candidates were examined the very creditable number of 205 qualifying for the badge and certificate.

One of the institutions of the Battalion was its conferences. These were held monthly at Battalion HG and presided over by the Commanding Officer and in his absence by the Second in Command Those attending were the four Company Commanders, the specialist Officers and the regular Staff. Adjutant and Quartermaster. One of the interesting things about these conferences was that we met in mufti and could therefore, without violating military law and discipline treat all questions raised, in an outspoken manner. Indeed, there were occasions when there were very candid exchanges of opinion and short but somewhat breezy passages.

Security was not the most outstanding attribute of these meetings, in fact they became so well known that during the last two years or so it was rare to attend a meeting without a visitor. Among the distinguished visitors were the Sub-District Commander—Col. Macartney; Sector Command—Col. B. Taylor Lloyd, M.C.; Col. Ernest Evans, K.C., Second in Command of Sector ; Lieut. Col. Hughes Williams, C.O. 2nd Cards. Battalion ; Major Tom Owen ; Col. Jarvis Jones ; Major Sam Davies of the 4th Carms.

Although never called upon to defend their area against the enemy, there were several incidents that gave the Home Guard chances of showing their knowledge and readiness. In the Summer of 1942 two suspicious characters were reported to a Platoon Commander in an adjoining Battalion area. Enquiries were made and at 1800 hours it was found that the two men had crossed to the 3rd Cards. area. The matter was reported to Battalion HQ., a message immediately sent from there to the Platoon concerned and the men were both traced and identified in a matter of thirty to forty five minutes. In May 1942 the following message was received at

Battalion HQ. at 1235 hours—" German paratroops dropping at Bwlchyllan." At 1240 hours another message came through to the effect that Paratroops were dropping at Cilcennin. At 1343 hours it was reported that the parachutists were practice ones from a neighbouring aerodrome. During that comparatively short period of 68 minutes all these preparations were made. The Commanding Officer, 2nd in Command and Acting Adjutant were at HG. where the C.O. took charge. Within fifteen minutes messages had been sent to O.C.'s 'B' Company, 'A' Company, Officer in Charge, R.A.S.C., 1st. Cards. Battalion and 2nd Cards. Battalion and O.C. Troops, Aberayron. A Despatch Rider was sent to HQ. 'B' Company and O.C. 'C' Company had St. David's College Mobile Platoon 'ready' with 75% muster plus the necessary transport. In addition, all reserve ammunition had been placed in bandoliers at Battalion Head Quarters.

From time to time bombs were dropped in the area. These were naturally of importance to the Home Guard and their reactions were in each case interesting and illuminating. With the exception of ' D ' Company all the others were concerned either with bombs in their own or in adjoining areas. Fortunately there were no casualties. Altogether a matter of about twenty bombs of various weights were reported in or near the Battalion area but in each case it was found that the Home Guard were ready and willing to undertake anything asked of them. On November 20th, 1940, one of the Observers at the Local R.O.C. post reported an aircraft travelling N.W. at 5,000 feet. He added that he could see a cross on the fuselage—the marking of a German Plane. Later the post was informed by Centre that the aircraft was hostile and had been shot down into the sea at Strumble Head, Pembrokeshire, a ' Junkers 88.' The following message was received:—" The Commandant at Pembrey wishes to congratulate the two men on duty who reported this aircraft and gave the correct direction and height". The observers on duty at the time were Mr. F. Selwood and Mr. Aeron Griffiths. The shooting down of this Junkers 88 happened after the heavy raids on Coventry but this was the only enemy bomber to be shot down over this country that day. Vide Press—" An enemy bomber attempting reconnaissance over the Midlands yesterday was shot down into the sea after a chase. It was the main incident in a day almost free of raids." On the 24th August 1942 at 8 p.m. a Liberator was seen approaching the post from the West travelling at a height of 2,000 feet. It was plotted in the usual way. At 8.40 p.m. the following message was received from a base via Centre —" Congratulations on your efficiency in plotting. The Liberator was the one in which the Prime Minister, the Rt. Hon. Winston Churchill, was returning to this country from Russia." The report from Lampeter was the first received since the Liberator appeared over land. The observers were Messrs. J. Rogers and Idris Sturdy.

On February 28th, 1944 a very sad incident occurred in 'B' Company area. At 2.30 p.m. Major R. G. Thornton while at the Railway Station, Felinfach, noticed black smoke rising above the Trichrug in the vicinity of Cross Inn. The Battalion HQ. was immediately informed by 'phone. Major Thornton accompanied by Signalman Rowlands, a Sergeant in the Special Constables and a qualified ambulance man proceeded to investigate. They took with them from Company HQ. the First Aid equipment and picked up Sgt. E. E. Evans, Home Guard and Mr. Noakes, both qualified first aiders. After a little search along the Trichrug it was found that a plane had crashed near Cross Inn. A car then arrived from Battalion H.Q. containing the Adjutant, Capt. C. C. L. Fitzwilliams, Sgt. Major Owen and Q.M.S. Cadman who had brought with them a stretcher and first aid outfit. There was then a very efficient Corporal of Police from the Radio Location Station in charge. When the plane (a Halifax Mark III) struck the ground, the petrol tank exploded scattering pieces of the plane over a wide area and setting on fire a haystack near Hafod Farm. Two of the airmen had baled out and were suffering only from superficial cuts and bruises. One was suffering from shock. They were both taken to the nearest house. By this time, twenty five Home Guards were present, who were at once organised in a circle around the place as small arms were still exploding. A report was then received that two of the crew had jumped either without parachutes or their parachutes had failed to open. Major Thornton took about twenty of the Home Guard to make a search while another party was sent to help N.F.S. to prevent the rick fire from spreading. The R.A.F. Corporal, Capt. Fitzwilliams and P.S. I. Owen searched the place for bodies, the remains being placed in charge of the Police who had then arrived with an ambulance. Major Thornton's party found the other bodies, making it possible now to account for the whole crew of seven. Major Talvan Davies in whose area the plane crashed organised a party of twelve to guard the site. Others who did excellent work in connection with this tragic occurrence were— Major P. J. Parrott and Private Morris of the Pioneer Corps.

Pte. Aelwyn Jones, Mark Lane Stores, spends his weekends at his home in the hilly fringe of the Battalion area. In September 1941 during a lovely moonlight Saturday night Pte. Jones was standing outside his home, listening to the melancholy drone of enemy aircraft passing overhead on their way to bomb Liverpool. There was nothing unusual in this, he had listened on many occasions before, but something unusual did catch his eye. He saw floating silently down to earth, about 100 yards away, a large parachute. He immediately proceeded to the field where it was expected to land to capture the enemy airman and thus to draw first blood for the Battalion. As soon as he got into the field, there was a mighty explosion and Pte. Jones was thrown violently down but was otherwise uninjured. He realised that he was chasing, not a German parachutist, but a land mine. A few seconds afterwards another heavy explosion occurred on the other side of the house. For the next few minutes Pte. Jones searched the sky for further parachutes but none were seen. He found his mother uninjured but the door and windows had been blown in and various pieces of crockery smashed. Considering the nearness of the explosions it is amazing that so little damage was done. The force of the explosions was distinctly heard in Lampeter 15 miles away and caused many windows to rattle. The incident is not without some compensation as Pte. Jones claims to be the first one of the Battalion to come under enemy fire. The doubtful honour of enemy damage to H.G. property fell to 'A' Company. A sea mine exploded on the shore near the H.Q. and blew in a plate glass window. The H.Q. staff maintain that this was an enemy mine but the absence of proof did not shatter the confidence in the claim.

One of the earliest incidents that caused widespread excitement occurred near Mydroilyn in early 1941. Information had been received that an enemy airman had been seen to bale out and land in a field. News spread with amazing rapidity and soon the whole countryside was alive with searchers from every organisation— H.G., Specials, A.R.P., the local farmers, school children and every regular soldier. A lorry load of police and soldiers armed to the teeth arrived from Aberystwyth. The search continued but no enemy airman could be found. Doubt as to the authenticity of the alarm was soon felt and after the initial excitement the facts were sifted and the source of the rumour traced. It transpired that the alarm originated from a small boy who thought he had seen a man jumping out of an aeroplane. Further enquiries cleared up the cause of all the excitement. An aeroplane was seen to hedge hop in the neighbourhood, appearing and re-appearing occasionally. At the same time a suspicious figure, carrying a sheet of corrugated iron on his back, was seen by the small boy who jumped to the conclusion that this might be an enemy airman; thus the alarm was raised and no one knew where it started except the small boy who was appalled at the activity and imposing strength of the local civil defence. He was too frightened to bring his knowledge to the authorities, but after two days of cross examination he admitted what he knew and the search was called off and all retired to their normal duties after two days of complete dislocation of normal routine.

As soon as rifles and ammunition were issued to the Home Guard our thoughts immediately turned to Capeli, near Lampeter, an old and disused rifle range. This range was constructed in 1901, soon after the Boer War and on the formation of the Pembrokeshire Imperial Yeomanry or P.I.Y., of which there was one squadron at Lampeter. There were three targets and firing points at 100, 200 and 400 yards. The range was soon put in some order and firing practice was held almost every Sunday during the whole existence of the Home Guard. Regular troops in nearby camps and the Americans at Highmead also used the range. It was a common sight to see 50 or more cars every Sunday on the Lampeter, Aberayron Road, near the Range. Other ranges were approved and used in each Company area, " D ' Company on the beach at New Quay, ' A ' Company also on the beach, ' B ' Company in the hills behind Tregaron. In addition to rifle ranges, there were miniature rifle ranges and grenade ranges almost in every section. It is worthy of note that during the whole existence of the Battalion there was no accident of any kind.

To qualify as a *sniper shot* was quite an ordeal and required good stamina and good lungs. To the young and active it presented no great difficulty but to the over 40's it was a real trial. It is interesting to note that in this difficult course only eight riflemen qualified for the whole Battalion. At the 300 yards firing point 13 rounds were issued to riflemen who were fully equipped in battle order. On the word 'go' they had to crawl over very rough ground in the approved style for fifty yards, and then run fifty yards to the 200 yard point, load, set the sight and fire five rounds in 25 seconds. Immediately after, they had to run to the 100 yard point in 30 seconds and fire five rounds again in snap shooting fashion, i.e. the target only appearing for five seconds and disappearing for five seconds. The remaining 75 yards proved a real trial of stamina. As this was over very rough ground, a number were allowed to run to within 25 yards of the target which only appeared for five seconds. During this brief period the exhausted men had to fire three rounds from the hip. Many tried this course, but few were called to receive their badges.

In addition to Proficiency Tests the Battalion Commander and the Company Commanders from time to time arranged exercises both to aid and test training. There were also exercises on more ambitious lines held by both Sub-District and Sector to test the defensive measures adopted by different Companies and Battalions, Islands of Resistance and so on. We will not weary the reader with details of these exercises but it is interesting to note how comprehensive these were in their scope. In each exercise, as has already been mentioned elsewhere, the co-operation of the A.R.P., the Police, and the N.F.S. was necessary and always available. Some of the combined Civil and Military Exercises were on the lines of, T.E.W.Ts. or " Tactical Exercises without Troops " where problems were set and answered. Here are some specimen problems from a T.E.W.T.:

Enemy forces are reported to be advancing in a particular direction. The authorities are unable to enforce the 'stand firm' policy, and stream of refugees in carts, on bicycles and on foot are streaming along the road which will shortly be required by military traffic moving along to deal with the enemy. Forward parties have been sent to contact police and keep the road clear. Problem I :— " Which authority deals with the Refugees ? and what steps will such authorities take to deal with the problem ? " Problem II :— Two lorries laden with Ministry of Food Supplies are mixed up with the stream of refugees. They bear E.L. Labels and drivers state they have orders to proceed to their destination as quickly as possible. What action is taken and by whom ? Problem III :— A man in civilian clothes who states that he is a Royal Naval Medical Officer returning from leave is stopped at a Road Block. What does Officer in charge Road Block do ? Problem IV :—A fracas occurs between refugees and soldiers who are at a road block, the three Home Guard and five civilians are seriously injured. Four civilians are seized by the troops—(a) How are the casualties dealt with ? (b) What happens to the arrested civilians ? Problem V :—The A.R.P. Controller makes a demand on the railway for coaches to evacuate refugees. At the same time the railway authority receives an order from the military to send engines and trains in the opposite direction for military purposes. The railway cannot do both. What do they do ? In six hours the position has changed. The enemy with the aid of aircraft has secured a bridgehead and bridges vital to military traffic have been damaged by air attack. Problem VI :—O.C. Troops decides he must have 300 men immediately to clear the obstruction. How does he get them ? Where do the necessary tools come from ? Problem VII :—He finds also that several houses must be demolished. All are occupied. No Royal Engineers are available. What is the procedure for evacuating civilians from these premises ? Who will carry out the demolition work ? Problem VIII :—Enemy troops are now within two miles of the town. Sector Commander considers the roads and bridges over the river should be demolished to hold up enemy advance. What action does he take ? Problem IX :—The Garrison Commander realised that sooner or later the town must fall. What arrangements does he make about (a) Food Stocks, (b) Immobilisation of telephone communications. Contrary to expectations the enemy advances on each side of this second town with the result that it is isolated. Problem X :—(a) In whose hand is the government of the town vested (b) What steps are taken to ensure fair distribution of food. Problem XI :—It becomes necessary to issue certain instructions immediately to the civil population in this isolated town. How is this done ? By this time another enemy force has landed on the Glamorgan coast; Llanelly and

Carmarthen having been seriously bombed. Problem XII :—The A.R.P. Sub-Controller at Llanelly finds that his resources are insufficient to cope with damage, rescue work and provision of drinking water. Communications with the County Controller have been broken down. Whom does he approach and what action is taken? Problem XIII :—N.F.S. Divisional Column Officers at Carmarthen report to Fire Force Commander that the fires are so serious that they cannot deal with them, The Fire Force Commander promises assistance in spite of heavy calls at Swansea. How does the Fire Force Commander implement his promise? Problem XIV :— Field Force Units are moving along the road towards Swansea. Who is responsible for ensuring that the roads are kept clear and what action will he take? Problem XV :—Another attack by enemy aircraft is made on Llanelly. Bombs containing a yellow liquid are dropped in considerable numbers. No casualties have been reported. What action is taken? (a) by the A.R.P. Sub-Controller, (b) by the O.C. Troops. Problem XVI :—A Police Constable observes 10 parachutes descending near his Village. What action does he take? Problem XVII :—A farmer, who is not a member of the Home Guard brings in two enemy parachutists tied up in netting in a cart. He says he shot one and these surrendered. Was he justified in his action? Problem XVIII :—A deputation of citizens approaches the Sector Commander and asks for arms to be issued to the Civil Defence Services. What is the reply of the Sector Commander? Problem XIX :—The Sector Commander asks the Duty Officer at Sub-Area for permission to close a Railway Block? What action is taken?

Exercises in Platoons were arranged to test their operational role, to test their communications up to Company H.Q., to exercise Company Signals and Intelligence Staffs and to practice co-operation with Special Police, Civil Defence and N.F.S. A typical report on an exercise of this kind by the Company Commanders was as follows :—1. Co-operation with Civil Defence Units, (a) The work of the stretcher party deserves all praise, (b) Individual members of each service have been taught to have liasion with other services. 2. Muster. Lack of transport hindered this—general muster was well tested, and found not excellent but satisfactory. The general response to the exercise is considered very good and promises well for the future. Similar exercises were held up to Company strength with similar objects in view, plus exercises in Battalion strength particularly for mustering purposes from time to time. In one of these ' muster ' exercises Battalion reported 587 on parade two hours after receiving message.

When in autumn 1943, the 112th Inf. Regiment of American Troops arrived at Highmead to complete their training for the invasion of Europe, the idea of a large scale exercise was considered.

This idea gave us a grand opportunity to test out defences and organisation, and to the Americans, an opportunity of trying conclusions with an 'enemy' differently dressed, whose tactics could not be read in any text book. For the Lampeter garrison it was an opportunity to put into practice against a really imposing force one of the several defence schemes which had been discussed over many many months. The exercise was carried out on November 28th 1943 and was called 'Lightening', and as it turned out, the weather gods seemed to resent the name, for the battle was fought on a cold wet and windy day with poor visibility. The battle was to take the form of a delaying action by the Home Guard

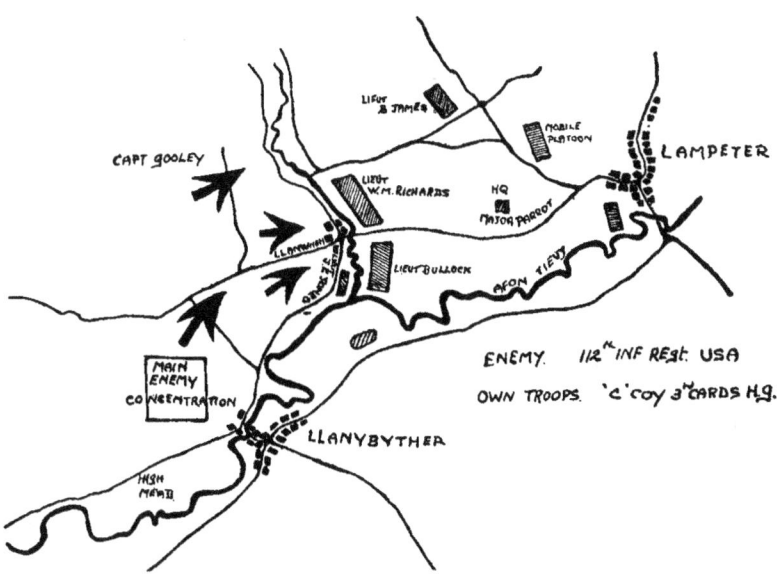

against vastly superior forces and was to be a 'full dress affair—nothing banned except live ammunition. The special constabulary under Inspector D. R. Thomas and the A.R.P. service under Professor D. Dawson nobly supported the Home Guard. In addition, various 'underground' bodies of men and women, including children gave valuable information and in several instances performed valiant deeds of sabotage. In fact, the whole countryside seemed to be organised for the destruction of the enemy. The Battalion Commander received information at about 9 a.m. that a very strong force was advancing up the right bank of the Teifi in the direction of Lampeter. This information was conveyed to the local garrison commander, Major Parrott, commanding ' C ' Company, who then assumed full control and acted as he saw the military situation at that time. This then was the appreciation of the military situation as he saw it.

On the 27th November, 1943 the enemy estimated to be about one infantry division, landed on the South Carmarthen beaches. They have advanced up the Towy Valley and one Battalion, which is the left flank of the Division, has been sent up to the Teifi Valley. At 0900 hours, the Centre of Resistance, Llanybyther, was subdued and information was received by the C.O. 3rd Cards. Bn. H.G. that the Battalion was advancing up the right bank of the River Teifi in the direction of Lampeter. Orders were given to the Military Commander of Lampeter to stop their passage at all costs until 1350 hours when regular troops would be able to come to the relief of Lampeter. The Battalion Commander advised the Military Commander of Lampeter to put as many mobile troops as possible, in the country between Lampeter and Llanwnen, and fight a rearguard action back to the town, being as aggressive as possible, but not to send more than 50 men across the River Granell. The Battalion Commander considered that the Smith Gun and all available M.Gs. and L.M.Gs. should be taken out of the Centre of Resistance, but bombards and northovers should be left in Lampeter for the final stand. Permission had been obtained from South Wales Division to blow bridges Co-operation with the A.R.P., N.F.S., Observer Corps and Mobile Ambulance had been established for information and sabotage work.

At 11 a.m. all defensive positions shown on the sketch were manned. Shortly afterwards contact was made with the advancing enemy. The heaviest pressure was experienced around the bridge at Llanwnen.

After inflicting considerable casualties, all positions were maintained, but after an hour the enemy, strongly reinforced, compelled the defenders to withdraw to their prepared positions.

The battle now developed into a rearguard action compelling the enemy to advance with great caution. Thus for the first hour of this important battle the enemy had only gained a matter of a few hundred yards on a very narrow front. It was now evident that the defence was being treated with the greatest respect. A probe here and there brought instant and accurate fire, which inflicted further casualties without much gain of ground.

Things continued developing in this way until the information was received by the defence that a new threat to Lampeter had developed.

Failing to make the necessary progress northwards, a Mobile Column was sent to try and outflank the defence. This column

moved along the Llanwnen-Cribyn road out to Maestir. That road was not without its defences. The enemy, paying scant attention to these defended points, rushed along and at great cost a few just managed to reach Lampeter before the arrival of the regular troops. In the meantime, the main H.G. force was unhurriedly withdrawn to Headquarters without losing contact with the attacks, and, owing to their perfect knowledge of the ground, without much loss. At the subsequent ' inquest' the 112th Battalion were high in their praise of the way the H.G. were handled and had done their work. In fact, their Officers were emphatic in their opinion that the honours in this battle were those of the defence. To us this was indeed a fine testimonial.

On the 30th September 1941 Lampeter and district took steps to set up Invasion Committees, consisting of representatives of the Home Guard, the Special Constables, the County Police, the A.R.P. Services and the Local Authority. Since Lampeter was the Regional Headquarters of all the services a regional committee was set up to organise the district. This Committee was made up of the Rev. T. Oswald Williams, Mayor of Lampeter (*Chairman*) ; Major Forbes (*Home Guard*) ; Superintendent Arnold Davies (*Special Constables*) ; Professor Daniel Dawson (*A.R.P.*), and Inspector Thomas Price (*County Constabulary*). The Committee visited and set up local invasion committees in the following places— Lampeter, Llanwnen, Alltyplaca, Llanybyther, Rhuddlan, Cwmsychpant, Cwrtnewydd, Gorsgoch, Drefach, Cribyn, Felinfach, Silian, Llangybi, Llanfair and Cellan. These Committees would only function in the event of an invasion, and they were to be focal points to give guidance to the civil population and to co-ordinate any necessary action affecting a number of services. The work of these Committees covered a wide field and included the co-ordinating of civilian plans with the military scheme of defence ; the enrolling of volunteers and the allotting to them of various tasks to help the military forces, e.g. digging trenches, and earth walls ; clearing or blocking roads, removing debris, doing first aid and burying the dead in the event of heavy casualties due to enemy action : (if there was need, compulsory enlistment would be carried out by the Ministry of Labour and National Service) ; the ascertaining of local sources of drinking water in case the usual supplies were interrupted ; cooking and distributing food to the military forces or civil defence services, and distributing food to civilian under the direction of the Ministry of Food and the taking of a census of tools available for such work as was needed and also stirrup pumps, sandbags and so on. We were spared the bitterness of invasion and these committees, established and ready, happily were never called upon to function. We had to envisage a time when certain parts of our country were in enemy hands with the possibility of failure of broadcast reception, with our telephonic communications cut, our daily newspapers undistributed or unprinted and many post offices in enemy hands. It would be more than likely that the enemy would attempt to mislead or alarm the civil population. The country was prepared for such an emergency, and the Ministry of Information was set up to forestall any such attempt and to foster the morale of the people. A County Information Committee had been set up at the commencement of hostilities, but on the 24th November 1942 six Emergency Information Officers were appointed for the County of Cardigan and one was established at Lampeter for the centre of the County and the Rev. T. Oswald Williams was appointed E.I.O. and Mr. I. G. Williams as his Assistant. The E.I.O. was to establish contact with the chief officials of the Local Authority, the Government departments and the Services. At the request of the competent authority the E.I.O. would secure publicity for urgent and essential notices. He was also to contact the local authority with a view to finding out its arrangement for emergency feeding in a post-blitz period. He was also by public meetings, showing of films etc. to keep the inhabitants informed of the true state of affairs in order to avoid panic and to bolster up the morale.

After the formation of 3rd Battalion, Invasion Committees on the above lines were set up in each Company Area with the Company Commander who was alsothe Military Commander, as Chairman. The above gives a fair idea of the amount of work and organisation involved.

The youngest of the specialised trained groups with Battalion was essentially Signals. Company Commanders not unnaturally felt that with the continual requests for specialists, the forces at their command were very seriously depleted for the really serious business of defence. However, under pressure from Higher Authority and with the consciousness that ' communications ' was an essential of successful offensive or defensive action, the Commanding Officer was successful in getting the services of an efficient Signals Officer, Lieut. Dixon, who in the short period of nine months made a very efficient Signal Section. The work of collecting and training Signals commenced in February 1944 and this is the report of training and attainments in October 1944.

Lampeter weather at its best, buses and motor cycles brought approximately 100 signallers to the town. The Signal Section, now nine months old, strong, sturdy and instructed, was to receive its ' standing down ' orders, its congratulations and badges from the C.O. The Army conducts examinations for signallers and grades the successful candidates under two heads (i) Proficient—those who are considered qualified to act in their particular branch of signalling

(ii) Classified—fully fledged signallers, entitled to wear the coveted cross-flags badge. Colonel Evans distributed 56 badges to ' classified ' signallers on October 22nd and qualification records to a further 19 ' proficient ' men and women. Yes, ' and women.'

When a wise government decreed that the Home Guard could avail itself of the services of women for non-combatant duties, here was clearly a heaven sent opportunity for the Signalling Section. A woman's place may doubtless be in the home or the canteen, mounting guard over the oven, but with her quick mind and facile tongue she is admirably suited for telephone and message work. 54 flocked to the colours and on 16th March, 1944, the Signal Section held its first mass meeting, in the Bryn Road School. Instructors from Sub-District and Sector H.Q. held classes in the four branches of Signals :—Phonogram (i.e. the transmitting of messages by telephone), Radio Telephony, Despatch Riding and Visual. A kindly, hardworking catering officer with his staff provided two substantial meals, for a signaller, whether Mr. Private or Miss Volunteer, is not unlike Napoleon's soldier in that he or she works or fights on his or her—No ! We cannot write ' stomach,' it would be indelicate. These instruction classes were held monthly and by June men and women were taking classification tests. Mere statistics are not very exciting but a few may be pardoned. On the roll of signallers there were 162 names ; 102 men and 60 women. 85 acted as Phonogram Operators, 26 as Radio Operators, 25 were despatch riders and 26 Visual Signallers. When the Signal Section stood down the classified and proficient signallers numbered 39 phonogram operators, 11 despatch riders, 3 R:T Operators and 22 Visual Signallers.

Another fertile source tapped by the Signal Section was the A.T.C. Here were Cadets already proficient in sending messages by morse and the Air Ministry permits them to enrol in the Home Guard for non-combatant duties. 25 A.T.C. cadets joined the Signal Section, 22 from the Wycliffe College Squadron. These 22 all classified as Visual Signallers.

A comprehensive system of communications was drawn up with Trichrug as the eye of the Battalion area. From this lofty windswept eyrie signallers transmitted messages to Felinfach by radio and to Lampeter, via Nanthenfoel, by Aldus Lamp. Every village which could boast of a H.G. Section could also boast two Phonogram Operators qualified to man (more usually to ' woman ') the village telephone. At Battalion, Company and Platoon Headquarters were despatch riders. The visual Signallers were detailed to man points between Trichrug and Lampeter so that, unless the enemy cut the telephone lines, drove despatch riders off the roads, spotted and removed various well-selected wireless and visual points, there was a reasonable chance that messages would flow freely through the

Battalion area in an emergency. The writer recalls an occasion in Battalion H.Q. when three distinguished heads were bent low over the map of the Battalion area—the Commanders of Sub-District and Sector and the 3rd Cards. Quarter Master. What operation plans, what impressions of our communications were passing through their august minds ! As they raised their heads, the eager signal Officer noticed that they had been studying, not the map but . . . comparing the respective merits of two fishing 'flies.'

At the end of July, as a changes from hours of theoretical study, the Signal Section held an extensive Exercise arranged in the form of a competition between the North and South areas of the Battalion. Messages were transmitted from village to village by Dispatch Riders, telephone and flags, returning to Battalion Head Quarters after being 'handled' by 12 pair of signallers. It speaks well for the signalling that errors were exceptionally few in the messages received. The visual operators, signalling across a valley by Aldus Lamp, showed commendable enterprise. The Lamp failed but the A.T.C. Sergeant in charge determined to get his message through. Breaking a branch from a tree, he tied the white shirt he was wearing to it and transmitted the message by 'Flag.' Lest any unrestricted reader should imagine that this transmitting of messages is a simple unskilled job, we ask you to picture 50 Home Guards not signallers but mere fighting men, sitting in a semicircle in the sunshine, 30th September. They were receiving a lecturette on the accurate passing of verbal messages. As an elementary test a message was started at both ends of the semicircle to be passed from man to man, received at the centre and the two messages compared. The original message ran ' Halifax bomber crashed at New Quay ; 6 men killed, 3 men rescued." The First message reached the centre as " Enemy bomber passed over New Quay at 11.30." The second group, excelled their companions with " Enemy plane passed over Halifax at 2.30." Not quite the original message. Royal Signals have played a vital part in winning the second World War. But why did not the Germans give us an opportunity of testing our Signals and communications ? Perhaps the answer is ' The Home Guard.'

Of all the various departments, the medical department was looked upon with the most affection but with the least attention. The Battalion Medical Officer, Major Alun Worthington, always acknowledged the fact that the medical side should not in any way detract from the aggressive efficiency of the Battalion. Major Worthington, fully realising the difficulties of a vast and sparsely populated Bn. area, devised a scheme where certain personnel in every section combined the duties of fighting men with those of medical assistance. For many years before the War, almost every village had its St. John's Ambulance Class, so that the rudiments of

First Aid to the injured were already known to a great many members of the Home Guard. Most villages also possess small kits of First Aid equipment, and on this basis the future organisation of the medical services was formed. The postponement of the impending invasion allowed the Battalion M.O. to perfect this branch of the Home Guard work, and as time went on, the removal of possible casualties was thoroughly understood by all within the Battalion and by the A.R.P. Service dealing with this branch of their work. The various Battalion exercises proved that the scheme was sound and workable. The Railway Staff, always experts in First Aid work, proved invaluable to the Medical Officer not only in forming part of the organisation but also in training new personnel. In the event of a casualty in the field, First Aid was rendered on the spot by a special squad in that Section, and he was removed, as soon as time and circumstances permitted, to a First Aid point determined by the Company Commander in conjunction with the A.R.P. First Aid Party, usually in a school, church hall or public building or, where this was not possible, a convenient spot in the country. The casualty was then conveyed by A.R.P. ambulance to a First Aid Post. These posts were situated respectively at Lampeter, Aberayron, New Quay and Tregaron and were under the direction of the Red Cross. The casualty rested here until he could be removed to Hospital. Should the casualties at any one spot be too numerous to be effectively dealt with by the H.G. and A.R.P. Services, one or more of the three mobile medical units in the County would be directed to the area to help relieve the situation. This system of treatment by the H.G. in the field, with quick evacuation by the A.R.P. service, proved to be quite satisfactory in the various exercises. But the work of the M.O. did not cease with the organisation of his department, he had to go to every platoon to give First Aid lectures and this in the winter and in the black-out proved to be no mean task. The proficiency test always included a test on First Aid to the injured and the number of successful candidates shewed its high state of efficiency in this respect. This efficiency was always coupled with genuine enthusiasm for the general war effort and the H.G. whether individually or in complete units rendered whatever help could in any sphere. In addition to holding the medical service ready for any emergency, the Bn. M.O. had to make provision in case of accidents at all larger scale exercises, firing practices, grenade throwing and trench mortar firing. At all important exercises an ambulance and a trained squad were always present.

In the beginning of 1943 an appeal was made by the Blood Transfusion Service for volunteers to become blood donors. Circulars, explaining the very necessary measure to save the lives of our soldiers sailors and airmen and also civilian wounded in air raids, were distributed in the various districts. The pamphlet explained that research had proved that thousands of lives had already been saved. Much more use of transfusion is being made and therefore a very much larger demand for donors. We were fortunate in this area in escaping the trials and dangers of enemy action and hitherto we had enjoyed comparative immunity from the terrible consequences of war. The response was excellent and in addition to individual donors, in some districts whole section of the H.G. presented themselves at the Transfusion Centre.

The Battalion Commander appointed Lieut. E. C. Evans as Catering Officer to be responsible to him for the feeding of his men. The Catering Officer firstly selected throughout the Battalion area suitable premises which were empty or occupied. He then discussed the object with the owner, and as soon as an agreement was reached, informed the Local Food Executive Officer and asked that the catering establishments at the selected addresses be registered for use in an emergency after mustering. This information was also passed on to S.D.Q.C. (Sub-District Quartering Commandant) for requisitioning purposes for War Office. Then throughout the Battalion area a selection of suitable tradesmen such as butchers, grocers, milkmen, bakers, etc. were appointed for registration by the Food Executive Officers as suppliers of rationed foods. In due course the Food Executive Officers issued a " Valid only in Emergency " notice and made arrangements for the selected tradesmen to receive sufficient supplies to enable them to meet demands as soon as requested. There was also an alternative source namely, R.A.S.C. Arrangements could be made to feed from the nearest C.S.D. (Command Supply Depot) as done by any Regular Army Unit but the 3rd Cards. Bn. worked on the former system. The opportunity must be taken here to thank the Officers Commanding C.S.D. for their help, guidance and co-operation at all times. Often when weekend operations were held in outlandish spots such as the beaches of Aberayron when hundreds had to be fed and commodities ran out owing to better attendance than was anticipated, the R.A.S.C. always came to the rescue with the encouraging assisance of all at the Depot. The Salvage section too should be mentioned for its contribution of fuel for fieldwork from its dump. It always recognised that, when the emergency came for mustering, it would be sudden and disorganisation inevitable, so to guard against this, each and every member of the Home Guard was told again and again to bring his first twenty four hour haversack ration with him, an order always remembered. A further precaution was taken by the Battalion H.Q. :—the storing of " 3 day R.A.S.C. reserve rations" and " forty eight hour packs," the latter consisting of sufficient tinned meat, tea, sugar, margarine, chocolate and biscuits to feed a proportion of the Battalion's strength. In certain military supply depots throughout the country a further reserve of food known as the " seven day pack " was stored as an emergency measure. So the position was a very healthy one in the 3rd Cards. Bn. area and supplies in registered establishments were periodically inspected by HQ. Officers.

Among the many things which were planned in advance were accomodation of feeding establishments, chairs, tables, fuel, cooking utensils, mess, orderlies, tables of quantities, recipes for dishes, bills of fare and finance and responsibility of instruction. Head Quarters adopted a scheme whereby whenever a muster took place, orderlies were supplied from various platoons to help to carry out the cooking, different ones were detailed each time, the result being that wherever an operation took place in the Battalion area, there were always members of the Home Guard who were used to handling utensils for cooking and producing a meal for their strength in that particular spot. When annual camps took place a great deal of instruction in field cooking was given. The Catering Officer insisted at all times on carrying out conditions as near as possible to regular army regulations and discipline, which proved very effective and was always appreciated by the rank and file. First class meals were produced (under very difficult conditions, very often) the proof being clean, cleared plates and satisfied soldiers ready to tackle the next task. Many amusing incidents took place at the gatherings which added to the efficiency of the Home Guard, unknowingly to themselves. Here is an example. The Catering Officer used to experience great difficulty in convincing members always to bring their knife, fork and spoon and very often had to carry about with him a vast supply for defaulters. This was becoming a very common practice and the same boys would forget to bring the utensils each time. However, at one week end camp a very fine dinner was produced—roast beef, roast and boiled 'spuds,' green peas and plenty of gravy (with an object). The same gang came up for knife, fork and spoon (about 20 to 30 in number) but were told " Sorry we have none for you today, you will have to cut them from the hedgerow." It was a pitiful sight to see them eat their very moistened dinner with their fingers but no more trouble was experienced in the Battalion with what is known as a golden rule in the army—" Never forget your knife, fork and spoon." This brief report cannot be closed without the Battalion's thanks to the co-operation and help given by the three Food Executive Officers in the area, without whose help great difficulties would have been experienced. Also the Headquarters staff who always gave of their best to a very noble cause.

Capt. W. T. Davies, Westeria, Llanybyther, who had charge of the Battalion ammunition, always contended that the subject was dry and dangerous but to the others was full of exciting possibilities [Possibly, the argument was the result of the very limited supply that we had to be satisfied with in early 1941]. Of course, the Battalion at first had to rely on private supplies for the ordinary shot cartridges, and the next stage was the acquisition of four boxes of ball ammunition containing three balls per cartridge. This type of shot was considered more effective than the ordinary cartridge used for shooting rabbits. Soon, however, all types of ammunition began to arrive from the small .22 bullet to the large 20 lbs high explosive mortar bomb and the question of storage was solved by the erection of the Nissen Huts. Two of these were for use as a Battalion reserve and the remaining four, one for each Company, were situated at Aberayron for 'A' Company, Felinfach for 'B' Company, Lampeter for 'C' Company and New Quay for 'D' Company. These large huts were soon filled up to the roof, and a careful inspection of the contents of the six huts was carried out by Capt. Davies every three months and a report submitted to Western Command. It is a matter of great satisfaction to every one and especially to the ammunition officer that no accidents due to faulty ammunition or to carelessness occurred, although on one occasion Capt. Davies trembled to think of what might have happened on one of his inspection tours. (On one occasion he found 24 grenades, primed and ready for action, under the bed in the home of a leader). At one time the Battalion had on charge twenty tons of bombs and fifteen tons of various types of ammunition. It is interesting to note that the Sten Gun fired a 9 .m.m. bullet of which there was a large supply from a captured Italian Dump. The 'Molotov Cocktail' became famous throughout the world and consisted merely of a beer bottle filled with petrol, rubber and phosphorus, and served many purposes. As supplies improved, the Molotovs were replaced by the Mills Grenade or '36'—a very serviceable grenade that could be thrown by hand or discharged from the E.Y. Rifle and the Northover Projector. The 'Thermos Flask' or '73' Grenade was a 4 lb. blast bomb and the '74' was the 'sticky bomb' used either for anti-tank work or demolition. The '65' or Hawkins Grenade was used to blow off the tracks of tanks. Tanks could also be dealt with by anti-tank mines of which there were four types. The only shell we possessed was the '3' inch shell fired from the 'Smith Gun.' The heaviest high explosive was however the 14 and 20 lbs. bomb fired from the Spigot Mortar. There were of course many other types with a special purpose.

In the event of 'the balloon going up' one of the many vitally important arrangements would be that of transport for troops and supplies. The 'earmarked transport scheme' was therefore drawn up by the War Office, by which every individual unit of the Home Guard was ensured of all essential facilities for transport and communications by means of lorry, car, and motor cycle. Owners of vehicles in the Battalion area were asked to place them at the disposal of the Home Guard in the event of an emergency and a special ' G ' Licence for each vehicle was prepared and held ready at Battalion Headquarters should such an emergency arise. At such a time no other private vehicle of any kind would be allowed on the road. By this Scheme the Battalion had at its command twelve heavy lorries, five cars and some forty motor cycles. In each case the owner had been served by the Transport Officer with a Certificate of Acceptance partly filled in but on which the final details (such as the amount of petrol in the tank) would be completed when the vehicle was brought to the central assembly point at St. Thomas's Square, Lampeter, and handed over to the Battalion. These vehicles had in every case been personally inspected by the Transport Officer, whose duty it was to ensure by periodic visits that they were kept in a state of good running order. At the same time Drivers were appointed by Company Commanders for the proportion of those vehicles allotted to them, whilst the remainder were to be assembled and held in reserve, to be disposed of as required in accordance with the nature and location of the emergency. In addition to all this earmarked transport the Bn. also had seven W.D. Motor cycles for specific purposes, such as Despatch Riding and Signals, and a W.D. Van and three cars were allotted to H.Gs. for general purposes. These were regularly serviced by one of the Lampeter garages. The experience of the French in 1940 had warned us of the urgent need to conserve supplies of petrol and at the same time render them inaccessible to the enemy. The Bn. held large reserve supplies at two central points in the Bn. area and instructions had been issued for the disruption, i.e., the temporary disablement, of petrol pumps and other plants, and also, in the event of extreme necessity, for the complete destruction of such plant by certain local Military authorities. These then, were the transport arrangements by which the 3rd Cards. Bn. was prepared, both offensively and defensively, to meet the challenge of the German invader.

The small savers of the British Isles played their vital part in the winning of the war. His Majesty the King was the Patron and Lord Kindersley the President of the National Savings movement. With the recollection of the Great War and its high interest rates, the Chancellor of the Exchequer, in his wisdom, decided to keep money rates as low as 3%. He was able to borrow the bulk of the money, required for the prosecution of the War, at a lower rate than 3%. At its peak, the cost of the prosecution of the War amounted to the colossal sum of £15,000,000 per day. The War Savings campaign was initiated with the dual object of preventing inflation, and the keeping down of consumption to a minimum, so that production could be directed as far as humanly possible towards the winning of the War. The Small Savings of the country averaged £12,000,000 and £15,000,000 per week, apart from the Special Efforts. Cardiganshire is sparsely populated but it played a noble part in the giving of its money towards the War efforts. The average per head ranked with the highest in the country and no small credit for this is due to the enthusiastic response of the local officials in charge of the Movement. Among these the name of Mr. William Lewis, J.P., Lampeter ranks very high. In the Battalion area the results of the Special Effort Weeks are tabulated as below:—

	Lampeter Area	Tregaron Area	Aberayron & New Quay Area
War Weapons Week	£106,470	£7,345	£86,169
Warships Week	£102,620	£34,150	£76,900
Wings for Victory Week	£79,425	£35,759	£79,380
Salute the Soldier Week	£104,353	£21,498	£110,587

During 1941 and onwards evacuees arrived in the area in small and large parties. The unofficial ones arrived in twos and threes to stay with friends and acquaintances, and this was done quietly and unobtrusively and therefore caused no comment other than a general impression that there were many new faces to be seen in the countryside. Soon official evacuees began to arrive in large parties, the first organised party of 350 children coming from Liverpool. Mr. Alwyn Jones, Chief Billeting Officer took over from the teachers who accompanied the children and without fuss very efficiently saw they were cared for. Another 250 arrived from Liverpool later to be followed by 200 from ' Bomb Alley.' The last party of 185 children came from Greater London whose homes had been bombed and destroyed.

The calling out of a large body of men requires a great deal of thought and organisation and particularly it requires ' secrecy.' In order to attain this, the Home Guard upon the receipt of certain ' Code ' words, known only to those in authority, had to carry out certain specific instructions. It can now be divulged what these code words were and the implications of each :—

1. *Arras*. A state of extreme tension exists and parachute landings at dawn or during moonlit nights, are very possible. At the same time maintenance of industrial output is of primary importance. An Officer to be at, or within close call of, each Battalion H.Q. and an Officer or O.R. at each isolated Company H.Q. both by day and night. Certain important posts must be manned, patrols furnished and inlaying picquets established, during hours of darkness and until one hour after dawn. Men should not lose pay or work because of

such duties, but it is important that until full light observation posts with means of communication should be manned. All Home Guards men to be warned that calling out is likely and the means of doing so completed. Arms, ammunition, medical supplies and tools located as required.

2. *Newton.* Invasion believed imminent and airborne landings, especially at dawn, are very likely. At the same time the importance of maintaining industrial output is so great as not to warrant the mustering of units. At night, action as for *Arras*, but essential garrisons of important posts, patrols and observation posts must be maintained until one hour after dawn, even if some loss of work or wages results. By day, observation posts manned, and at least three men on all important posts irrespective of their missing work if reliefs cannot be arranged. Compensation up to a maximum of 12s. od. per day, subject to an over-riding maximum of £3 10s. od. in any one week, for actual loss of wages by men necessarily so employed, may be paid by Battalion Commanders, vide A.C.I. 1272:41. The issue of *Newton* will usually mean that STAND TO has been issued by G. H.Q., Home Forces for Western Command.

3. *Action Stations.* Invasion imminent. Earmarked vehicles necessary to complete units to the scales authorised will be taken up. Any additional guards necessary for important points including certain Regional and Civil Defence H.Gs. will be posted either for day or for day and night duty. Compensation for loss of wages payable as for *Newton*. The issue of ACTION STATIONS means that regular troops are placed at full readiness and that Home Guard in other Commands have been mustered.

4. *Oliver.* Hostile action has occurred or is believed to be of such imminence as to warrant the mustering of one or more Home Guard Battalions, irrespective of the disturbance of war production and distributing services involved. All personnel of the unit or units to which issued will be called out, posts manned and reserves located according to pre-arranged defence plans. Exceptions to the call out will be previously designated personnel engaged in railway operating, pumping and similar essential services, who will NOT be called up until the situation makes the continuance of their normal duty impossible. The uniform and arms of such personnel, if not worn, will be kept where they can be taken into use at the shortest notice. District H.Gs. will notify T.A.As. as to which units have been issued with *Oliver* and men who report for duty may be paid at a rate up to 12s. od. per day on their application.

5. *Oliver* will be used in accordance with the following, in order to obviate the risks of surprise by the enemy. Owing, however, to the grave interference with war production and distributing services, reference will, when this is possible without serious delay, first be made to H.Q. Western Command.

(i) It will usually be issued by H.Q. Western Command to all or some of the Battalions in Districts or Sub-Areas specified.

(ii) It may be issued, at his discretion, by a District or Sub-Area Commander either to all Battalions or to certain Battalions only (for example all rural Battalions might be issued with *Oliver* while urban Battalions remained at *Newton*).

(iii) In sudden emergency, and when communication with Sub-Area H.Q. is not readily possible, it may be issued by any Sector Command for all, or certain of, his units, or by a Home Guard Battalion Commander or a regular C.O. for his own, or the nearest Home Guard Battalion.

(iv) When *Oliver* is ordered, the complete Battalion will be mustered and H.Q. Western Command will be notified if the order was not issued therefrom.

(v) A Battalion when once mustered will not be unmustered except by order of H.Q. Western Command. Personnel found to be surplus to requirements, as shown by the development of the situation, will be given, by their Battalion or Company Commander, leave of absence for periods not in excess of twelve hours. They will be notified as to where to report at expiration of leave and will remain in uniform, or keep uniform at hand, and be ready to turn out if called for while on leave. (This should enable factory and other production to continue if operations are not in progress.)

In April 1944 the Battalion Commander found it necessary, in view of the military situation, to call a parade of all the Battalion Officers at Felinfach. The muster was 100% and looking back at events that pushed each other so quickly off the stage, it is at any rate interesting to note that Higher Authority, even as late as April, 1944 did not consider the country safe from invasion. Supporting the Battalion Commander at this parade were Col. B. Taylor Lloyd, M.C.; Lt. Col. Ernest Evans, K.C.; Lt. Col. J. Jarvis Jones; Major Tom Owen and Capt. Sam Thomas, all from Sector Headquarters. These were the instructions issued on this one and only total Officers Parade :—

"I have called this parade for a very special reason which I am sure you will presently appreciate. When the Home Guard was formed our Country was in a state of extreme peril. Since that exciting time, we have been allowed to proceed with our training unmolested. We have been allowed to prepare ourselves and adjust our plans to meet an emergency that we knew would one day come along. That emergency is now imminent. Nobody knows how imminent. If you are not absolutely satisfied that your plans are sound and in good working order, now is the time to rectify them, and not next week. The bomber that crashed in 'A' Company's area last

Tuesday night might have been an enemy one. It might have been a troop carrying plane. There might have been half a dozen of them. Are you all perfectly satisfied that you could have dealt with a situation of that nature? Here I would like to compliment Major Thornton on the splendid way he dealt with the emergency. At 1507 hours it was reported to him that it was thought a plane crashed. He saw smoke over the crest of a hill. His prompt reporting enabled the situation to be effectively dealt with. Both the Sub-District Commander and the Sector Commander have asked me to communicate their pleasure at the prompt action taken by all members of the Home Guard who re-acted so promptly to the situation. The subsequent work was expeditiously and thoroughly carried out and great credit is due to every member of the party. I am quoting this as an incident admirably carried out. The people concerned were on their toes and ready. The recent issue of arms and ammunition has no doubt given you a clue that the Home Guard may be required to go into action in the very near future. The Sector Commander will give you up to date information of the present state of affairs. Don't forget what security means. The inspection of your identity cards shows that greater care must be exercised. The ' G ' Licence is an authority signed by myself and must be carried out. You will see that every man must carry his civilian card and signed, it is useless not signed. Beware of rumours and fifth columnists. You should know how to deal with them. The Company Commanders and the Signals Officer have been overhauling our communications during the last few days. You are responsible for all communications in your platoon areas and I must know without delay that your means of transmitting and relaying information is 100% in order. Women can be enrolled in the Home Guard for telephone service and the A.T.C. and H.G. Cadets can be enrolled as messengers. The Catering Officer has recently been satisfying himself that reserve supplies of food are held and are in good order. Your men will be responsible to provide their own rations for the first twenty four hours. The Packs must not be used without authority from me. You are to satisfy yourselves that your system of calling out your men with the least delay possible is 100% efficient. Each man must know precisely what he must do and where he is to go on Action Station. Orders will be issued to you through your Company Commanders in mustering and what guards, inlaying pickets he may require. No special transport will be provided to meet the sudden emergency, but you will earmark suitable lorries, cars and vans in liaison with the Police to meet your requirements. These must not be confused with transport, which is earmarked by Battalion in the case of general mustering. Your mobile fighting platoons should be in training and should be ready for immediate action. It is important that you should be in close liaison with the Police, A.R.P., Civil Defence and the Royal Observer Corps. You are to make yourselves immediately acquainted with the question of ammunition and reserve supplies for all weapons including your personal weapons and sub-artillery weapons. If you have no revolver you should provide yourselves with stens. Be sure that every man knows how to protect himself against gas. Gas masks will be carried on mustering, on other occasions as instructed by your Company Commanders. You will see that casualties are initially treated and then transferred as soon as possible to the A.R.P. Services who will be responsible for their care. Remember, you are first and foremost a fighting force with a job of work to do. Inspect all arms and ammunition frequently and see that they are ready for immediate use.

From now on I shall expect a 100% parade once a week and serious training with a definite and immediate object is to be your motto. Company Commanders will call a Conference of their Officers and senior N.C.Os. as soon as possible to ensure that the machine is in good running order. Be sure that you know the essentials of writing and transmitting messages. It is your primary duty to see that all information is transmitted at once. Remember that I can only act on the information that I receive. Situation reports, even if there is nothing to report, must be rendered at intervals stated by your Company Commanders. You need not worry about the men's pay. The organisation for this is complete and ready to function at a moment's notice. These are some of the most important facts I want you to remember and to keep constantly before your minds until the emergency is over. This is not a reading of the Riot Act, because I know full well the splendid work you have already done, but it is a reminder that we should all see that our allotted task will be honourably carried out.

At the end of August there were 1,085 Battalions of the Home Guard in Britain, excluding Northern Ireland, with a total of 1,727,095 men. The number of women Home Guard Auxiliaries was 30,696. These hitherto secret figures were revealed by the War Office recently. The activities of the Home Guard have been distributed over the field of coastal defence, motor transport, light anti-aircraft, bomb disposal and infantry. There are now 7,000 men working with Regular coastal batteries and 141,676 in Regular Light A.A. Batteries. Anti-aircraft defence, the War Office considers, has been the most important contribution of the Home Guard to the war effort. Of the 7,000 employed in this country on bomb disposal duties not one has lost his life. Other duties in which the the Home Guard have distinguished themselves include the rounding up of escaped prisoners of war and the rescue of crews trapped in crashed British aircraft. A Staff Officer at G.H.Q. Home Forces told me that the original intention was to form a force of only

150,000 strong, but in answer to Mr. Eden's broadcast appeal on the night of May 14, 1940, 400,000 men had volunteered within a fortnight. The Home Guard have earned the following decorations for Gallantry, 2 George Crosses ; 13 George Medals ; 1 O.B.E. ; 11 M.B.Es. ; 6 B.E.Ms. ; and 58 commendations. For other services, 31 C.B.Es. ; 87 O.B.Es. ; 139 M.B.Es. ; and 107 B.E.Ms. ; The whole Battalion are justifiably proud of the fact that one of the 139 M.B.Es. awarded was to Second in Command Battalion— Major D. M. Evans. Capt. Enoch Davies was also awarded a decoration, namely, the Territorial Decoration in recognition of 20 years' meritorious service in the Territorial Army. Those, who tried to get an issue of any kind to which he was not entitled, will agree that Capt. Davies fully deserved this award.

The Great Day had arrived—December 3rd, 1944—the day that we had all looked forward to, the day when we could ease our labours and relax from our Home Guard duties, but at the same time a day of parting with old associations. When the official date of the Stand Down became known, preparations were immediately set on foot for the final parade. A week of feverish activity at the Bn. H.Q. and Company H.Qs. brought us to the eve of December 3rd when everything was staged to the last detail. Much had been completed —buses ordered, routes planned and money obtained for this last subsistence allowance. A livestock lorry was to bring both ponies and riders from the wild country beyond Tregaron. Dawn broke on Sunday in a distressing manner and it was evident we were in for a cold, wet and stormy day. The parade was originally planned to take place in the beautiful setting of the College Field, but fortunately alternative plans had been arranged for the ' Common.' Soon after 10 a.m. in pouring rain, buses started arriving and there was a steady stream of men making for the ' Common.' By 10.45 about 600 men had already taken up their position by their markers. The Battalion was drawn up in Companies with the Flag Party, Bn. H.Q. Mounted Troops and the Women's Auxilliaries as separate group. Major D. M. Evans handed over the Parade at 10.55 to the Commanding Officer, Lieut. Col. J. Albert Evans, M.C. Shortly afterwards the Sector Commander Col. B. Taylor Lloyd, M.C. and his staff arrived marching by him. A short religious service was conducted by our Chaplain—Rev. S. E. Bowen and this was followed by an inspection by Col. Taylor Lloyd, M.C. and Col. Jarvis Jones, the Sector Training Officer, both taking the opportunity of bidding goodbye to as many officers and men as time permitted. During this time the weather was at its worst and the rain came down in torrents. The Sector Commander and his staff proceeded to the Saluting Base in front of the Town Hall and the Commanding Officer marched the Battalion through the Town. The Flag Party led, and was followed by the H.Q. Company, 'A' Company, The Aberystwyth Cadets Drum and Fife Band, 'B' Company with its Mounted Troops, 'C' Company, 'D' Company and lastly the Women Auxilliaries. The 'eyes right' was given to the Sector Commander in front of the Town Hall. The Flag Party then took its position near the Saluting Base, and the Battalion, except the band, who joined the Flag Party, marched on and took up a position on both sides of the road and facing each other. The Flag Party, led by the Band, now marched down the entire length of the Battalion for the last time and proceeded directly to the Parish Church.

In the meantime, the Battalion had marched back to the Common to form up again. This was the last opportunity the Commanding Officer had of addressing the Battalion.

Before dismissing he said :—"This is the last opportunity I have of addressing you as a Battalion and I do so with a grateful sense of having had the priviledge of commanding a group of men and women who had the highest ideals of service and loyalty.

" We have had the Order to ' Stand Down,' but that does not mean that our duty as a Battalion is at an end. We are still on duty. It is, therefore, necessary that we keep our uniforms and our organisation in serviceable condition until we get the Order to disband.

" We pray that that moment is not far distant—when we can rejoice in the knowledge that we have served to the best of our ability those men and women who are serving us so gallantly. I would like to acknowledge the work done by my 2nd i/c—Major D. M. Evans, who has spared nothing to make this Battalion efficient and happy.

" I also gratefully acknowledge the splendid work done by those hard worked and harassed officers—the Company Commanders and also those Officers with special duties.

" I also take this opportunity of thanking all members of my permanent staff for unfailing courtesy and loyalty at all times.

" And to every Officer, Non-commissioned Officer, man and woman in this Battalion I offer my sincere gratitude.

" There are three organisations whose guidance, ungrudging help and great patience have helped to create in this Battalion an atmosphere of great friendliness—I refer to Sector H.Q., Sub-District H.Q. and the T.A.A.

" And finally I would like to mention the help and co-operation so readily given by the Police, Special Constables, all branches of the A.R.P. Services and by the public generally in every parish of my Battalion area.

" Each one played a proud part in the grand design during the period of great peril.

First Official "March Past Jubilee Review",
Aldershot, July 9th, 1887,
18 years.

SERGT. G. BROOKS
D. Company, 3rd C.O.S.

Final "March Past" H.G. Stand Down, Lampeter,
December 3, 1944.
76 years.

" One final request I have to make of you, as your Commanding Officer—When Peace comes, Play your Part.

" I hope to have the opportunity of thanking each one of you personally on some future occasion and in the meantime ' Au Revoir '."

With the command—" Fall out the Officers, Battalion dismiss "— ended four and half years military service that has periodically been necessary since the time of Alfred the Great. The C.O. then returned to the Parish Church to join the Flag Party under the Command of Lieut. James, senior Platoon Commander of ' C ' Company. The party was representative of the Battalion, comprising 1 Officer and 2 O.Rs. of each Company and Sgt. Major Owen. The party marched slowly down the aisle to the chancel steps where the C.O., taking the flag, addressed the Vicar—" This Flag I deliver into your hands for safe custody within these walls." The Vicar acceded to the request by saying—" I accept this Flag for safe custody within this Church." The Vicar then took the flag and placed it on the Altar. The National Anthem was followed by the Benediction and so ended a little ceremony that closed the final chapter in the history of the 3rd Cards. Bn. Home Guard. The Flag at our request will hang in an honoured place in the Parish Church for all times as a reminder of the great peril the Country suffered during the second world war.

Home Guard parades were held throughout the length and breadth of the land on that day; and representatives from every H.G. Unit from the Orkneys to Lands End and from the Wash to Cardigan Bay gathered together in London and marched past the King and Queen six abreast. From all parts of the British Isles and Northern Ireland they came to march past His Majesty the King, the Colonel-in-Chief of the Home Guard. He stood at the Salute in Hyde Park, and around him were grouped the Military Attaches of the United Nations, representatives of the Dominions, and the Chief Leaders of the Army, Navy and Air Force. 7,000 gave him the 'eyes left' as he stood at the Salute for 40 minutes. Among them were three H.Gs. from the 3rd Cards. Bn. H.G.—L/Cpl. T. Owen ("B" Company), Pte. Williams ('D' Company) and Pte. W. G. Griffiths ('C' Company). They were chosen to represent us at the final parade.

The men marched through the West End of London on a three mile long route lined with cheering crowds. The long procession was headed by a detachment of five Metropolitan Policemen on grey horses, then followed by detachment after detachment of Home Guard six abreast, including eleven Home Guard bands. The cheers grew in volume as the head of the column gave a smart ' Eyes Left ' to the King whose right hand was raised in Salute.

Then for another forty minutes the march went on up to the saluting base, past the marking flags held by two rigid Coldstream Guardsmen, past the massed banks of people and out of sight towards Marble Arch.

People had begun to take up positions in Hyde Park to see the parade as early as 5 a.m. Daybreak hawkers and sellers of flags and favours did a brisk trade. Flags sold at 1s. each and souvenir programmes were 6d. each to the public and half price to the troops and children. Our three men were loud in their praises of the arrangements made for them and they said that they will never forget their experiences.

In the evening the Lord Mayor of London invited 200 Officers and N.C.Os. representing every county in Great Britain and Northern Ireland, but none of our men were successful in the draw for this function. They were, however, successful in being chosen to attend a gala performance at the Royal Albert Hall to be entertained by the best artists in the Country.

At 9 o'clock in the evening the King, broadcasting his thanks to the Home Guard, said :—

"Over four years ago, in May 1940, our country was in mortal danger. The most powerful army the world had ever seen had forced its way to within a few miles of our coast. From day to day we were threatened with invasion.

"In those days our Army had been gravely weakened. A call went out for men to enrol themselves in a new citizen army, the Local Defence Volunteers, ready to use whatever weapons could be found and to stand against the invader in every village and every town. Throughout Britain and Northern Ireland the nation answered that summons, as free men will always answer when freedom is in danger. From fields and hills, from factories and mills, from shops and offices, men of every age and every calling came forward to train themselves for battle. Almost overnight, a new force came into being, a force which had little equipment but was mighty in courage and determination.

"In July, 1940, the Local Defence Volunteers became the Home Guard. During those four years of continuing anxiety that civilian army grew in strength, under the competent administration of the Territorial Army Associations, it soon became a well-equipped and capable force, able to take over many duties from regular soldiers preparing to go overseas. I believe it is the voluntary spirit which has always made the Home Guard so splendid and so powerful a comradeship of arms.

"The hope that this comradeship will long endure was strong in me this afternoon while many thousands of you marched past me in one of the most impressive and memorable parades that I have ever seen.

"For most of you—and, I must add, for your wives too—your service in the Home Guard has not been easy. I know what it has meant, especially for older men. Some of you have stood for many hours on the gun sites, in desolate fields or wind-swept beaches. Many of you, after a long and hard day's work, scarcely had time for food before you changed into uniform for the evening parade. Some of you had to bicycle for long distances to the drill hall or the rifle range.

"It was well known to the enemy that, if he came to any part of our land, he would meet determined opposition, at every point in his advance, from men who had good weapons and, better still, who knew how to use them. In that way the existence of the Home Guard helped much to ward off the danger of invasion. Then, too, our own plans for campaigns in many parts of the world depended in our having a great citizen force to help in the defence of the homeland. As anti-aircraft and coastal gunners, sentries at vulnerable points, units for dealing with unexploded bombs, and in many other ways, the Home Guard have played a full part in the defence of their country. Many will remember with special gratitude the unsparing help given to the Civil Defence Services in days and nights of terror and destruction.

"But you have gained something for yourselves. You have discovered in yourselves new capabilities. You have found how men from all kinds of homes and many different occupations can work together in a great cause and how happy they can be with each other. That is a memory and a knowledge which may help us all in the many peace-time problems that we shall have to tackle before long.

"I am very proud of what the Home Guard has done, and I give my heartfelt thanks to you all. Officers, non-commissioned officers and men, you have served your country with a steadfast devotion. I know that your country will not forget that service."

* * *

The Home Guard stands down to-day, and His Majesty the King, in a special Army Order, sends them the following message :—

"For more than four years you have borne a heavy burden.
"Most of you have been engaged for long hours in work necessary to the prosecution of the war or to maintaining the healthful life of the nation ; and you have given a great portion of the time which should have been your own to learning the skilled work of a soldier.

" By this patient, ungrudging effort you have built and maintained a force able to play an essential part in the defence of our threatened soil and liberty.

" I have long wished to see you relieved of this burden ; but it would have been a betrayal of all we owe to our fathers and our sons if any step had been taken which might have imperilled our country's safety.

" Till very recently a slackening of our defences might have encouraged the enemy to launch a desperate blow which could grievously have damaged us and weakened the power of our own assault.

" Now, at last, the splendid resolution and endurance of the Allied armies have thrust back that danger from our coasts. At last I can say that you have fulfilled your charge.

" The Home Guard has reached the end of its long tour of duty under arms. But I know that your devotion to our land, your comradeship, your power to work your hardest at the end of the longest day, will, discover new outlets for patriotic service in time of peace.

" History will say that your share in the greatest of all our struggles for freedom was a vitally important one. You have given your service without thought of reward. You have earned in full measure your country's gratitude."

GEORGE R. I.

Colonel-in-Chief.

Officers of 3rd Cards. Battalion Home Guard at Stand Down.

HEADQUARTERS.

Commanding Officer	Lieut. Col. J. A. Evans, M.C.
Second in Command	Major D. M. Evans.
Medical Officer	Major A. T. Worthington.
Adjutant	Capt. C. C. L. Fitzwilliams.
Quartermaster	Capt. E. Davies.
Intelligence Officer	Capt. J. E. Lloyd.
Liaison Officer	Capt. Jos. Davies.
Catering Officer	Lieut. E. C. Evans.
Gas Officer	Lieut. Ezer Evans.
Ammunition Officer	Capt. W. T. Davies.
Signals Officer	Lieut. T. S. Dixon.
Chief Guide	Lieut. H. A. Harris.
Transport Officer	Lieut. K. C. Bird.

'A' COMPANY.

Company Commander	Major T. Talvan Davies, M.C.
Second in Command	Capt. A. Davies.
Platoon Commander	Lieut. J. W. Evans.
Platoon Commander	Lieut. R. M. Marter.
Training Officer	Lieut. D. O. Davies.
Platoon Officer	Lieut. J. E. E. Jones.
Platoon Officer	Lieut. W. Meredith Williams.
Platoon Officer	2nd/Lieut. James Robinson.
Quartermaster	2nd/Lieut. W. G. A. Bowen.
Intelligence Officer	Lieut. J. D. H. Parry.
Platoon Officer	2nd/Lieut. D. Morgan Jones.

'B' COMPANY.

Company Commander	......	Major R. G. Thornton.
Second in Command	......	Capt. J. E. Rogers Lewis.
Platoon Commander	......	Lieut. Joshua Davies.
Platoon Commander	......	Lieut. W. M. Richards.
Platoon Commander	......	Lieut. Evan Evans.
Intelligence Officer	......	Lieut. E. Jones Evans.
Quartermaster	......	Lieut. G. Edgar Jones.
Training Officer	......	Lieut. E. A. Thomas.
Platoon Officer	......	2nd/Lieut. T. J. Davies.
Platoon Officer	......	2nd/Lieut. Evan Davies.

'C' COMPANY.

Company Commander	......	Major P. J. Parrott.
Second in Command	......	Capt. G. L. Reade, M.C.
Training Officer	......	Lieut. E. J. Lewis.
Intelligence Officer	......	Lieut. J. A. George.
Quartermaster	......	Lieut. J. L. Jones.
Platoon Commander	......	Lieut. Ben James.
Platoon Commander	......	Lieut. W. A. C. Bullock.
Platoon Commander	......	Lieut. J. E. Jones.
Platoon Officer	......	Lieut. D. W. Evans.
Platoon Officer	......	2nd/Lieut. D. P. Davies.

'D' COMPANY.

Company Commander	......	Major D. E. Phillips.
Second in Command	......	Capt. Wm. Thomas.
Training Officer	......	Lieut. C. G. Meager.
Platoon Commander	......	Lieut. David Davies.
Platoon Commander	......	Lieut. Thos. Davies.
Intelligence Officer	......	2nd/Lieut. D. E. Thomas.

BATTALION AREA 3rd CARDS.

SCALE

KEY:
- ▨ A COY
- ▦ B "
- ◪ C "
- ▧ D "
- ♟ Observation Posts
- 1 Lampeter Golf Links
- 2 Trichrug
- 3 Cross Hands, Mydroilyn
- ⌇⌇ Highland over 1000 feet

Llan—
Aberarth
ABERAYRON
NEW QUAY
Llanarth
Dihewyd
Synod Inn
Llangranog
Talgarreg
Aberporth
Cartneny
PEMBROKESHIRE
CARDIGAN
LLANDYSUL
CARMA—

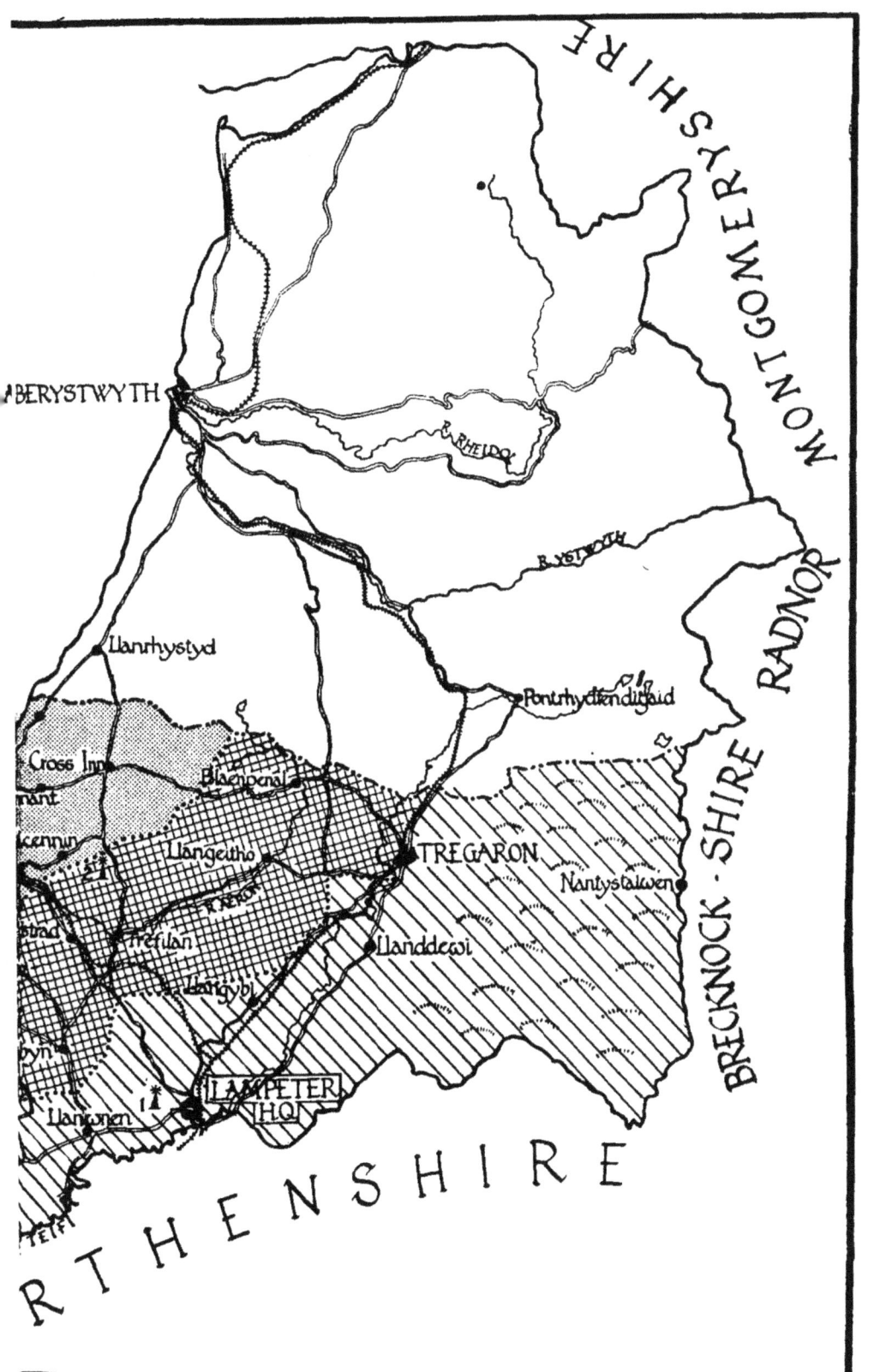

www.ingramcontent.com/pod-product-compliance
Lightning Source LLC
Chambersburg PA
CBHW070550090426
42735CB00013B/3136